and God said...

Science confirms the authority of the Bible

DR. FARID ABOU-RAHME

40 Bea… …tland

ISBN No. 0 946351 65 1

Printed by: Bell & Bain Ltd, Glasgow

CONTENTS

Acknowledgements

I extend my deep appreciation to:
the Institute for Creation Research and in particular the works of
Dr H. Morris and Dr D. Gish;
Mr Timothy Mellish for designing the figures in this book;
Mr Tom Wilson and Dr Bert Cargill for their editorial work.

Dedicated to

my wife Ilham
whose encouragement and support made this possible
my son and valued practical assistant Nabil
and my daughters Lina and Rula.

About the author:

Farid Abou-Rahme was born in the 'Holy Land'. He received his first two degrees in Civil Engineering from the American University of Beirut-Lebanon. After a period of work in the Middle East, he moved to the UK where he obtained a PhD degree from Sheffield University.

Searching for answers, the author spent years researching the subjects of *Science and the Bible, Creation or Evolution*. This research confirmed the authority of the word of God in every field it touches upon. He is keen to share this to strengthen faith in the Bible, and to present the Creator who became the Saviour of the world at the cross of Calvary.

Dr Abou-Rahme gives lectures and preaches on the subject, showing how science confirms the accuracy and the authority of the Bible. His booklet *Creation or Evolution; Does Science Have the Answer?* has been translated into several languages.

And God said... has been translated and printed into Arabic, Rumanian, Russian, Simplified Chinese and Portugese. Work is going on for Classical Chinese, Spanish, Slovak and Polish.

PREFACE

The Bible from beginning to end consistently states that the universe and everything in it were created by God, a God of infinite power and wisdom. "Without Him was not anything made that was made" (John 1:3). Yet throughout history, alternative views about origins have been propounded. Some of these, from ancient times, are classed as mythological, and people smile at them because they are so grotesque. Others, of more recent origin, have been classed as scientific, and many people take them seriously because they feel they are respectable and academic and rational. But are they? And what is the real reason why people wish for an alternative to creation?

This book explains clearly how the most popular of these theories, evolution, is neither logical nor rational nor scientific. Evolution does not follow good common sense, and it is not good science either! It has not been tested and proved experimentally as all proper science must be. It is a complex hypothesis which has been put together by extrapolation of some data away beyond the boundaries of their applicability, and by much wishful thinking and confusing jargon. It is a proposed theory, not an established fact. It has been modified and revised many times (e.g. Darwinism and neoDarwinism), but the trouble with the theory of evolution is that it has been accepted and retained in spite of *contrary* evidence, and lack of proof or rigorous test. It has been widely acclaimed and eagerly subscribed to because, as many students have said to me, "The alternative (God) is unacceptable and impossible!" It has been propagated as fact whereas it is fiction.

It is not that science has disproved the existence of God - it cannot and could not do this - but rather that so many scientists (and non-scientists too!) do not want to acknowledge the existence of God to whom by definition they would be accountable. Evolution theory has become the great excuse, and has supported a progeny of other theories like relativism, humanism, materialism, and of course atheism. The practical results of these are evident in today's societies all over the world. It is tragic to observe what happens when people "did not like to retain God in their knowledge" (Rom 1:28).

For a long time, many Christians felt that the threat of evolution theory was one they could not answer or cope with. Attitudes varied from refusal to consider it or face it, to compromise by adjusting the meanings of Bible words, or even abandoning some passages of Scripture. (How could they decide which?) One result of increasing access to higher education for the past two generations is that there now exists a substantial number of Christians who are able and willing to face head-on the challenge of these atheistic theories. Many have studied both pure and applied science in detail and in depth, are acquainted with its methodology, its ideas, and its limitations, and can write and speak authoritatively on matters where traditionally a clash and a contradiction have been perceived between science and the Bible. The author of this book is one of these scientists, and shows that in fact "Science confirms the authority of the Bible". Young people who have doubts about this will find many of their questions answered here.

On all continents today are to be found many scientists who are Christians. Their testimony is that real science does not undermine belief in the Bible in its entirety, submission to God and His authority, and faith in Christ and His dependability. The traditional view of the arrogant scientist pouring scorn on the Bible has not been abandoned in the world, for some scientists wish to retain that stance. But that view is without logic, and has less and less credibility as more and more young people especially, with an open and unbiased mind, are discovering the remarkable agreements between the facts of science and the revelation of God in the Bible.

Having taught university degree courses in chemistry for over 30 years, having researched and published extensively in scientific journals, and having had the opportunity of lecturing to many classes of students on the compatibility of science and the christian faith, I am very pleased to commend this book to a wide readership, young and old. Material like this will educate and enlighten enquiring minds, answer and rebut unfair and unfounded criticisms, and challenge and convict souls who are searching for the truth, searching for meaning, searching for God. He has revealed Himself in Christ, and to know Him is to know what is supremely worth knowing. Evolution leaves people groping in the darkness, without purpose, without direction, without hope. To find Christ and to know Him is to find the answer to life's most important question and quest: it is to have eternal life (John 17:3).

Robert W Cargill, BSc, PhD
Senior Lecturer in Chemistry
University of Abertay Dundee,
Scotland

INTRODUCTION

The authority of the Bible as the perfect word of God has been challenged throughout the ages. Recently, the challenge has been escalating at an exponential rate. The source of this challenge has been an increasingly aggressive "scientific" lobby attempting to promote the theory of Evolution as scientific fact. The image of confidence, which true scientists have built up with the people in the past, is being exploited by today's so-called scientists, to present their *false* science.

Paul writing to Timothy, nearly two thousand years ago, warned him against the "... oppositions of science *falsely* so called, which some professing have erred concerning the faith" (1 Tim 6:20-21) [1].

As a young person, I was taught to respect the authority of the Bible as the perfect word of God. Born in a christian home, I knew about the Lord Jesus Christ at a very early age, through the teaching and the life of godly parents. Memories of my father, who is now with the Lord, are of a man of faith who lived close to his Saviour; a real friend of God, who, as he sat in his chair with an open Bible, always had something to share about his wonderful Saviour. My mother was, and still is, a woman of prayer. Watching her live every word she preached, I could feel that her greatest desire in life was that all her children would come to a personal knowledge of her Saviour. All this had a great impact on my life and I wanted to know their Saviour. Their prayers were answered as I, the youngest of their children, accepted the Lord Jesus as my own personal Saviour at the age of twelve.

As I grew up, my faith and understanding of the word of God grew, and the problems that faced me grew also. One problem was difficult to handle: science and the Bible. Almost all my teachers and professors claimed that science had proved the Bible wrong, and that one cannot be educated and still believe in God and the Bible. I knew the answers must be there and I had to find them. Thus I started my long journey of searching for answers. I asked other Christians who had science degrees and the issues became more complex.

I found out that when the theory of Evolution started becoming popular in its early days, Christians panicked. Compromise solutions were formulated in haste in an effort to incorporate evolution into the Bible. This was accomplished almost always at the expense of the accuracy of the word of God. In many cases some professing Christians went so far as rejecting parts of the Bible, such as the first eleven chapters of Genesis in order to please the "scientific circles"!

There was no way I could accept this. My faith was based on the word of God, and I was sure of my salvation. Therefore the Bible must be true and perfect throughout from Genesis to Revelation. Either the Bible *is* the word of God which means it must be perfect, or it is not, in which case I don't need it. As far as I was concerned, it was all or nothing.

I spent years researching the subject. At school I was fascinated by science. I found similarities between science and my christian faith. Geometry, one of the most logical and perfect subjects, is based on axioms. These are statements which are self-evident and logical but cannot be proved. Similarly my christian faith is based on two axioms: God exists and the Bible is His word, both self evident and logical.

I was fascinated by experiments in the laboratory. One in particular was uniting chlorine, which is a poisonous gas, with sodium, a reactive metal. The result is sodium chloride (salt), useful and necessary for man. I saw similarities with my faith: human nature poisoned by sin (chlorine gas) uniting with the Saviour by means of His work at the cross of Calvary, and the result is a *new* creation (salt); "Ye are the salt of the earth!" (Matt 5:13).

Studying the subject of science and the Bible, and reading the works of other believers who accepted the authority of the word of God in all the subjects, I found amazing facts about the Bible that made me want to share them with as many people as possible : with believers to strengthen our faith in the word of God and with non-believers to challenge them with the claims of the Lord Jesus in the Bible: "Ye must be born again".

Why Science ?

People often ask me : "Why science? Is not faith enough?" Of course faith is enough. We are saved by faith. But it is faith that is based on the solid word of God. "Through faith we understand that the worlds were framed by the word of God" (Heb 11:3). The word of God challenges every believer : "...be ready always to give an answer to every man that asketh you a reason of the hope that is within you" (1 Pet 3:15). We are instructed to give answers!

Our children come home with all sorts of questions related to evolution and if we do not have the answers to satisfy them they may soon lose interest in the Book which, according to all their teachers and colleagues, contradicts science. Let us not fool ourselves and say we should tell them to believe and forget about what they are taught, because this is not good enough for students today, if ever it was. Of course they need faith, but they need faith in a perfect Book that can stand any test because it is the word of God the Creator. And unless we give them answers concerning this very important issue we shall continue to see the young people drifting away from our local churches.

Similarly, if we believers do not accept the literal inspiration and accuracy of the word of God in every detail, and that includes the first eleven chapters of Genesis, we will never experience the full blessings that are promised to us by God.

Why do I spend so much time on this subject? Three reasons come to mind:

1. The Lord has used this subject to reach many lost souls who do not ordinarily attend a standard church meeting or read a religious book. As part of my lectures, I always present a clear gospel message about the Creator who became our personal Saviour at Calvary. Thank God for the number of people who have come to know the Creator as their own personal Saviour when the evolutionary barriers, which Satan spent years building between them and the word of God, came tumbling down.

2. Evolution has caused problems to many believers, especially young people, whose faith in the authority of the Bible has been shaken or shattered by the claims of false science and the lack of practical support they get from other believers. To see the change in their faces

after they listen to the evidence, makes the effort more than worthwhile. Many young people write to me, telling how trusting the authority of the word of God has given them new boldness in their witness for Him. They have become bold and outspoken, presenting the Bible and their testimony openly to all those around them, whereas once they were ashamed to defend their faith. This calls for praise to our Creator and Saviour.

3. Lastly, I feel thrilled every time I read about a scientific discovery and find how wonderfully it agrees with the Bible record and how clearly it contradicts evolution. This reminds me of the words of the Psalmist: "The heavens declare the glory of God; and the firmament sheweth his handiwork", and "When I consider thy heavens, the work of thy fingers, the moon and the stars, which thou hast ordained; What is man that thou art mindful of him?" (Ps 19:1; 8:3-4). Indeed He is greatly to be praised.

Consequently, I believe that the Lord has called me to a ministry in this field. Over the years, as I have studied this subject, the Lord has taught me to accept *everything* that is in the Bible without interpreting it to suit my own ideas and opinions, whatever their source may be.

We shall consider three main aspects of the subject in this book: Science and the Bible; Creation or Evolution; and Evidence for the Flood and Noah's Ark. The concluding section will be devoted to the spiritual lessons that the Lord taught me as I studied this subject.

REFERENCES

1. *The Holy Bible,* King James Version: Cambridge University Press , UK, 1981.

(All quotes from the Bible in this book have been taken from this reference version.)

PART 1 - SCIENCE AND THE BIBLE

Chapter 1
AMAZING SCIENTIFIC FACTS

We are urged to search the Scriptures (John 5:39). If we do that looking at the subject of science, we find many examples of modern scientific facts, recorded in the Bible thousands of years before scientists discovered them. These statements were written by those who knew nothing of modern science, "but holy men of God spake as they were moved by the Holy Ghost" (2 Pet 1:21). "For whatsoever things were written aforetime were written for our learning", "that ye might believe that Jesus is the Christ, the Son of God; and that believing ye might have life through his name" (Rom 15:4; John 20:31).

We shall consider a few of these examples:

Physics

"He hangeth the earth upon ***nothing***" (Job 26:7).

Job wrote this fact over 3500 years ago and yet this is twentieth century physics. The Laws of Gravity which Newton discovered do not add anything to what Job recorded, they simply explain *how* God "hangeth the earth upon nothing"! At the turn of this century scientists believed that a space substance called "ether" existed throughout space and somehow helped to hold the earth in its position. But this has now been disproved, and the most scientific statement is still that "He hangeth the earth upon *nothing*".

This same Creator who "hangeth" the earth on nothing was willing to be "hanged on a tree" (Act 5:30) to secure forgiveness of sins for all those who believe in Him.

"He that sitteth upon the *circle* of the earth" (Isa 40:22).

About 700 BC Isaiah recorded this amazing fact. The word "circle" in the original language gives the meaning of "spherical". More than two thousand years after Isaiah, in 1519 AD, Magellan the famous navigator sailed around the world to disprove the belief that the earth was flat and proved what had been there in the Bible for over 2000 years, that the earth is round.

A spherical earth is also implied when in Luke 17 the Lord Jesus described His return by saying "in that day" (v.31) and "in that night" (v.34). This means that simultaneously it will be light on one side of the globe and dark on the other side. "In that day, he which shall be upon the housetop, and his stuff in the house, let him not come down to take it away... I tell you, in that night there shall be two in one bed; the one shall be taken, and the other shall be left" (Luke 17:31,34).

Astronomy

"The host of heaven cannot be numbered" (Jer 33:22).

Some further examples of the authority of the word of God exist in the field of astronomy. For centuries there have been attempts at counting the number of stars. Ptolemy counted 1056, Brahe said 777, Kepler counted 1005. The number has been increased until today it is well known that there are well over 100 billion stars in our own galaxy, with probably another 100 billion galaxies! Yet thousands of years ago Jeremiah wrote: "The host of heaven *cannot* be numbered". Even more amazing are the words of Ps 147:4-5; "He [God] telleth the number of the stars, he calleth them all by their names. Great is our Lord and of great power: his understanding is infinite". The same God who "made the stars also" is interested in each individual, as the next verses of this Psalm tell us.

Medicine and Public Health

"If thou wilt diligently hearken to the voice of the Lord thy God ...

I will put none of these diseases upon thee..." (Exod 15:26).

These laws given to Moses are modern twentieth century medicine and public health guidelines. God told His people not to eat "unclean" animals and this is still applicable today. The pig and the hare are exceptions, but modern medicine tells us that these two animals have parasitic infections that cause diseases if not cooked well, something which was very difficult to do as the people journeyed in the desert! God also forbade eating the flesh of any animal that had died a natural death, advice which is still enforced in most civilised countries today.

The principle of quarantine was also unknown until recently, yet God explained it to Moses nearly 3500 years ago. This ensured that contagious diseases which were spreading amongst other people who did not have God's laws, were perfectly controlled amongst the people of God.

The subjects of water supply and sewage disposal are today considered to be of extreme importance for public health and prevention of disease. Moses, however, thousands of years ago, was using the principles of bacteriology. He forbade the drinking of water from small or stagnant pools, or water contaminated by coming in contact with animals or meat (Lev 11:29-36). Directions for disposal of sanitary sewage by burial (Deut 23:12-14) and regulations concerning personal hygiene were far ahead of practices even in the civilised countries until the past century. Indeed "the eye of the Lord is upon them that fear him, upon them that hope in his mercy; to deliver their soul from death, and to keep them alive in famine" (Ps 33:18-19).

Haematology

"For the life of the flesh is in the blood" (Lev 17:11).

Over the ages scientists argued about the "life of the flesh", and suggested that various organs in the human body carried this responsibility. Blood was never on their list. In 1628, Harvey proved that the blood circulates from the heart and back to it, reaching all parts of the body via arteries and veins. He was the first to discover what is a well known fact today.

More recently, the sciences of haematology and immunology, two of the most rapidly expanding fields, have confirmed the fact that the sophisticated fluid we call blood, is uniquely life-sustaining. Scientists can spend a lifetime learning about various constituents of the blood, and the wonders of this life-sustaining fluid continue to amaze the human intellect.

"The life of the flesh is in the blood", although written thousands of years ago, is a scientifically sound and accurate statement. When blood is shut off from any organ or group of cells, the result is the death of that organ or group of cells. This is the pathophysiology of strokes and heart attacks. Cells can neither function nor live without the circulation of blood.

The life-maintenance of all cells, including brain cells, is dependent on the provisions of the blood. We now know that blood provides these cells with the life-sustaining substances (oxygen, glucose, amino acids) and takes away their toxic metabolites (carbon dioxide, lactate, urea). If these toxic substances are not cleared from the cells, they will eventually lead to their death. What an amazing system: the life of the flesh is *indeed* in the blood!

"Unto him [Christ] that loved us, and washed [lit: *cleansed*] us from our sins in his own blood" (Rev 1:5).

Despite our conception of blood, it is one of the most effective *cleansing* agents. This cleansing process described above is a by-product of an exchange mechanism whereby the blood trades with the cells, life for death.

The science of haematology helps us understand the amazing parallel truth in the Bible: "Unto him [Christ] that loved us, and washed [lit: *cleansed*] us from our sins in his own blood". This is not poetic language, this is a spiritual fact describing a dynamic spiritual exchange process similar to the physical. When Christ shed His blood for you and me on the cross, He took our sins and sinful nature upon Him: "who his own self bare our sins in his own body on the tree" (1 Pet 2:24), so that when we accept Him as Saviour and Lord we can be cleansed from our deadly evil and are able to receive His life.

"The blood of Jesus Christ his Son cleanseth us from all sin" (1 John 1:7).

Blood also cleanses the heart. When a clot blocks any of the arteries that carry blood to the heart, life is endangered. Cardiologists attempt through angioplasty to remove the clot in order to allow the blood to flow to the cells of the heart, otherwise the death of these cells is imminent. The Bible says "the heart is deceitful above all things and desperately wicked" (Jer 17:9). But His blood can cleanse the wickedness of the heart, if we allow Him to remove the obstructing clot by asking Him into our hearts. We then receive His eternal life. This is salvation: when the clot is removed, the blood flows and life is given.

Molecular Biology

"I will praise thee; for I am fearfully and wonderfully made" (Ps 139:14a).

It is fascinating to read about developments and discoveries in molecular biology. The DNA molecule is an outstanding example of the greatness of our Designer. Scientists used to think that the simple cell was really simple, until modern research started scratching the surface of the complexity of the DNA molecule, which is itself only part of the cell!

The efficiency of the DNA molecule as a carrier of information has been compared to the megachip. If the information in the world's libraries were to be stored with the aid of megachips, we would need a pile of them higher than the distance between the earth and the moon. If, on the other hand, it is stored on DNA molecules, 1% of the volume of a pinhead would be sufficient for this purpose! DNA is 45 million million times more efficient than man's 'hi-tech' silicon devices [1]. Indeed we are "fearfully and wonderfully made" by a great God!

Chemistry

"For dust thou art, and unto dust shalt thou return" (Gen 3:19).

In the late eighteenth century scientists developed techniques for analysing minerals, and many other such techniques exist nowadays. Chemical analysis of the composition of man's body, and of the dust of the earth, has shown that the following elements which make up the major constituents of the human body are also present in typical samples of dust on the surface of the earth:

Calcium	Oxygen
Phosphorus	Chlorine
Potassium	Carbon
Sodium	Hydrogen
Magnesium	Nitrogen
Iron	Sulphur

This shows that man is as the Scriptures first described him thousands of years ago "...he remembereth that we are dust" (Ps 103:14).

God has even provided nature with minute undertakers, whose purpose is to bring about the degradation process by which the "dust" is returned to the earth: "Then shall the dust return to the earth as it was: and the spirit shall return unto God who gave it" (Eccl 12:7).

Atomic Physics

"But the day of the LORD will come as a thief in the night; in the which the heavens shall pass away with a great noise, and the elements shall melt with fervent heat, the earth also and the works that are therein shall be burned up. Seeing then that all these things shall be dissolved, what manner of persons ought ye to be in all holy conversation and godliness" (2 Pet 3:10,11).

Who told Peter the fisherman that the atom can be destroyed, resulting in great noise, fervent heat and terrible destruction? This was discovered almost 1900 years after Peter recorded it (Einstein's formula $E = mc^2$). The description of the atomic bomb explosion at Hiroshima and various nuclear tests, give the details exactly as Peter recorded them.

The word melt is better translated from the original Greek as "to loose". This implies that the chemical elements will be burnt up because of the letting go of the nuclear forces that bind the protons and neutrons together in the atomic nucleus. This can be understood by the fact that the Bible tells us that Christ is "upholding all things by the word of his power" (Heb 1:3), and He is the sustaining power: "... He is before all things, and by him all things consist [lit : *are held together*]" (Col 1:17).

At present, the Lord Jesus is still the sustainer of the universe and upholds all things by the word of His power. He holds the atoms together and the universe in place. But on the day of the Lord, the atom will lose its binding forces, resulting in a tremendous release of energy and all that Peter describes in vv. 10-12.

Hydrology and Meteorology

1. The Earth's Wind Systems

"The wind goeth toward the south, and turneth about unto the north; it whirleth about continually, and the wind returneth again according to his circuits" (Eccl 1:6).

The science of Hydrology and Meteorology is a modern subject taught at many universities today, yet Solomon about 3000 years ago set out some basic principles of this subject. The above verse describes three phenomena about the wind, namely that:

(a) it circulates between the equator and the two poles, discovered by Hardley in the seventeenth century;
(b) the whirling about indicates the Coriolis force discovered in the nineteenth century; and
(c) the wind has specific circuits, discovered only recently.

We read about the wisdom of Solomon but "... behold a greater than Solomon is here" (Matt 12:42).

2. The Water Cycle

"All the rivers run into the sea; yet the sea is not full; unto the place from whence the rivers come, thither they return again" (Eccl 1:7).

The idea of the complete water cycle was not accepted until the sixteenth and seventeenth centuries. Yet more than two thousand years before the discovery, the Scripture in Ecclesiastes indicated a water cycle.

The water cycle is also described in the book of Job: "For he maketh [draweth up] small the drops of water: they pour down [distil in] rain according to the vapour thereof: which the clouds do drop [pour down] and distil upon man abundantly [the multitudes of mankind]. Also can any understand the spreadings of the clouds, or the noise [thunderings] of his tabernacle?" (Job 36:27-29). The passage summarises the phases of the water cycle: evaporation, condensation, and precipitation; corresponding remarkably to our modern understanding of this recent science [2].

Hydraulic Forces

"Make thee an ark of gopher wood: ... and this is the fashion which thou shalt make it of: The length of the ark shall be three hundred cubits, the breadth of it fifty cubits, and the height of it thirty cubits" (Gen 6:14-15).

Consider the dimensions that God gave in Genesis for Noah's ark, a powerful and fascinating demonstration of the supremacy of the Bible. In an experiment carried out at one of the most modern hydraulic laboratories in the world [3], models of twelve of the most famous ships including Noah's ark were placed in a huge tank and subjected to a simulation of the actions of tidal waves and currents similar to the roughest conditions at sea. At the end of the experiment, every single model ship had tumbled over except one : Noah's ark, designed by God, built by Noah over 4000 years ago, superior to the most modern human designers who claim today that they don't need God anymore!

General Science

"For the invisible things of him from the creation of the world are clearly seen, being understood by the things that are made, even his eternal power and Godhead; so that they are without excuse" (Rom 1:20).

As a final example let us look at the concept of the Trinity: God the Father, God the Son, and God the Holy Spirit being one God, which is ridiculed by most scientists.

The doctrine of the Trinity is that of God the Father, the unseen source and cause of all things; God the Son, who tangibly and visibly reveals the Father to man and who executes the will of God; God the Holy Spirit, who is unseen yet reveals God the Son to men through the media of other men and the Word which He inspired, and who makes real in the hearts and lives of men the experience of fellowship with the Son and the Father. All are equally eternal and equally God.

The physical universe (which should reflect its Creator) helps us understand the concept of the Trinity to an extent commensurate with our finite minds.

All things in the universe can be classified under *three* headings: ***space, matter*** and ***time***.

Space as we can comprehend it, although one entity, consists of three dimensions: length, height and breadth. The mathematical argument against trinity is that 1+1+1 =1 cannot be correct. This can be readily answered from mathematics and space that to get the cubical content or volume of any confined space, one has to multiply the three dimensions, and 1 x 1 x 1 = 1.

Matter involves three basic phases, each distinct from the other, yet each involves the whole matter: energy, motion and phenomena.

Energy is first in a logical causal order, but not in order of importance or precedence. Motion, which embodies and reveals and is begotten of energy, is the second. Phenomena proceeds from motion and comprise the ways in which motion itself touches and affects men, as the Holy Spirit reveals the Son and, through Him, the Father to men.

Time is one continuum also, but consists of three states: past, present and future. Each contains the whole of time, yet is distinct, and cannot exist without the other two. The future is the unseen source of time and is embodied and made real in the present. The past then proceeds from the present, becoming invisible again, yet continually influencing us with regard to the present and even, to some extent, the future.

There are so many things in creation, despite the fall, that reveal the beautiful attributes of God the Creator and even more wonderful revelations in His precious word, so that man is indeed without excuse.

The Holy Bible

"But the word of the Lord endureth for ever" (1 Pet 1:25).

To sum it all up, the Bible is the perfect word of God : "All scripture is given by inspiration of God" (2 Tim 3:16). It is an authority on every subject it touches upon whether spiritual or scientific. Let us take it as it is, and not interpret it to suit our own desires and ideas. Let us keep in mind that God says exactly what He means.

If there are things we do not understand, let us not try to find ways around them and compromise with the world, but rather accept them because "holy men of God spake as they were moved by the Holy Ghost" (2 Pet 1:21). There are many things we cannot understand with our finite minds, but one glorious day we shall understand it all as we shall see our Saviour face to face. Until then let us hold fast to our faith in Him, not giving Satan any chance to tamper with the word of God or plant doubt in our hearts through his channels of false science. Let us hold fast to the Bible, the word of our Lord and Creator; study it and obey it because it is perfect.

REFERENCES

1. Rosevear, D. *Creation Science*, New Wine Press, England, 1991, p. 43.
2. Morris, H.M. *The Bible and Modern Science*, Moody Press, Chicago, 1968, pp. 7-8.
3. *Acts & Facts*, Institute for Creation Research, El Cajon, CA. Vol. **22**, No. **9**, September 1993.

Chapter 2

TRUE SCIENTISTS WHO BELIEVED

As a general rule, it is taught today that if you are a scientist then you cannot believe the Bible. The word of God is attacked at almost every school, college and university around the world under the cover of science.

Yet if one studies the history of science and reads about those true scientists who invented something worthwhile, one cannot but marvel at the fact that so many of them believed in God or were true Christians.

We shall consider some examples of great scientists who believed.

Johannes Kepler (1571-1630)

Described as "the man who began the process that replaced superstition with reason" [1] for his great work and discovery in the field of astronomy, his three laws of planetary motion set the scene for modern astronomy :

- each planet moves about the sun in an orbit that is an ellipse;
- planets travel faster when closer to the sun;
- the square of the periods of any two planets' revolutions are in the same ratio as the cubes of their mean distances from the sun.

He summarised his faith by saying: "I am a Christian". He acknowledged God as "the kind Creator who brought forth nature out of nothing" [2]. His laws of planetary motion were a result of his faith in a God of order and not of chaos. In his book *Harmony of the Worlds*, published in 1619 to record his third principle of planetary motion, Kepler wrote: "Great is God our Lord, great is His power and there is no end to His wisdom" [3].

What Kepler said in later life reflects the christian faith this great scientist had: "I believe ..only and alone in the service of Jesus Christ...In Him is all refuge, all solace", and "I had the intention of becoming a theologian... but now I see how God is, by my endeavours, also glorified in astronomy, for 'the heavens declare the glory of God'" [4].

Robert Boyle (1627-1691)

As well as being the pioneer of modern chemistry, he contributed greatly to the advancement of scientific thinking. Amongst other famous discoveries, his work on the relationship of pressure and volume of gases is still known today as Boyle's Law.

Boyle saw no conflict between science and his christian faith. He wrote religious books which included a collection of christian devotions where he described simple observations from nature to illustrate christian truths. He had a strong faith in Jesus Christ as his Saviour and Lord. He wrote about Christ's "passion, His death, His resurrection and ascension, and all of those wonderful works He did during His stay upon earth, in order to confirm mankind in the belief of His being God as well as man" [5].

Sir Isaac Newton (1642-1727)

He was one of the greatest scientists, responsible for so many discoveries like the Laws of Gravity, Laws of Motion, and Calculus. His contribution to the advancement of science spanned the fields of physics, mathematics and astronomy.

Newton loved God and believed God's word. He studied the Bible and wrote books about his Bible study. He wrote: "I have a fundamental belief in the Bible as the word of God, written by men who were inspired. I study the Bible daily." [6] His view as a scientist was put clearly when he said: "Atheism is senseless. When I look at the solar system, I see the earth at the right distance from the sun to receive the proper amount of heat and light. This did not happen by chance" [7].

As Newton investigated the movement of the planets, he saw the hand of God at work. He expressed it: "This most beautiful system of the sun, planets, and comets, could only proceed from the counsel and dominion of an intelligent Being ...This Being governs all things ...as Lord of all" [8].

Michael Faraday (1791-1867)

He was a pioneer in the then unknown field of electricity. He was responsible for inventing the electric generator and electric transformer. He also built one of the earliest electric motors. His work in this field has been recognised in the naming of the unit of electrical capacitance, the farad.

Faraday was a Christian who lived a life filled with God's power. He remained humble, despite the fact that he had lunch with Queen Victoria, and that members of the royalty attended his lectures. He was an elder at his local church and he frequently preached the gospel. When asked by a reporter about his speculations concerning what happens after death, he answered: "Speculations? I have none. I am resting on certainties. 'I know whom I have believed and am persuaded that he is able to keep that which I have committed unto him against that day'" [9].

Samuel Morse (1791-1872)

He invented the telegraph and the Morse code named after him. The words of the first official telegraph message ever sent were chosen from the Bible: "What hath God wrought" (Num 23:23).

Morse was a Christian who made sure to give the glory to his Lord. He described his life's work as : "It is *His* work... 'Not unto us, but to thy name, O LORD, be all the praise'" [10]. He saw no conflict between science and Christianity.

Figure 1: Scientists who Believed

Matthew Maury (1806-1873)

He was a leading figure in the fields of oceanography and hydrography. He wrote famous articles and books amongst which some became the most popular textbooks in the field. He strongly advocated and gave advice on the Transatlantic Cable project, the first enormous breakthrough in world communication.

Maury was a devoted Christian who accepted God's authority over his life. He used his great achievements to bring glory to God whom he acknowledged as Lord of all creation, "whether of the land or of the sea". He was keen to defend his use of the Scripture in his research and in his writing: "I have been blamed by men of science... for quoting the Bible in confirmation of the doctrines of physical geography. The Bible, they say, was not written for scientific purposes, and is therefore of no authority in matters of science. I beg pardon! The Bible is authority for everything it touches. ... The Bible is true and science is true, and therefore each, if truly read, but proves the truth of the other" [11].

James Joule (1818-1889)

He was famous for the work he did in the field of physics relating heat to mechanical motion, hence giving his name to the unit of energy, the joule. He was also responsible for Joule's Law, as well as being one of the founders of the then new science of thermodynamics, providing the experimental basis for the famous First Law of Thermodynamics (which implied that the universe could not have created itself).

Joule was a Christian whose faith was well known. He saw great harmony between his work and the truth found in the Bible. Many of his fellow scientists shared this view and the rejection of Darwinism which was then sweeping England. Consequently, in 1864 in London, 717 scientists signed a remarkable manifesto entitled *The Declaration of Students of the Natural and Physical Sciences* affirming their confidence in the scientific integrity of the Holy Scriptures. Joule believed firmly in God as Creator and he set out his priorities: "After the knowledge of, and the obedience to, the will of God, the next aim must be to know something of His attributes of wisdom, power and goodness as evidenced by His handiwork" [12].

Louis Pasteur (1822-1895)

He established the new science of microbiology and bacteriology. He invented vaccination, immunisation and pasteurisation which has helped to save the lives of many. He was also responsible for the Law of Biogenesis which says that life can only come from life, contradicting the then fashionable evolutionary idea of spontaneous generation.

Pasteur did not find any conflict between science and Christianity. He firmly believed that "science brings men nearer to God". As an outstanding scientist he observed evidence of design rather than chaos. He said: "The more I study nature, the more I stand amazed at the work of the Creator" [13].

William Thomson (Lord Kelvin) (1824-1907)

He is well known for formalising the science of thermodynamics and formulating its first law (originally proposed by Joule) and second law in precise terminology. Both laws render evolution unscientific. He discovered the absolute temperature scale whose units were given the name Kelvin in his honour. He patented about 70 inventions during his lifetime.

Kelvin had a strong faith in God. He said: "Overwhelmingly strong proofs of intelligent and benevolent design lie around us... the atheistic idea is so non-sensical that I cannot put it into words" [14]. He saw no conflict between science and the Bible and believed that "with regard to the origin of life, science... positively affirms creative power" [15].

James Clerk Maxwell (1831-1879)

His electromagnetic theory and its associated field equations paved the way for twentieth century physics.

Maxwell was a devoted Christian who studied his Bible and was a church elder with a faith and commitment well known amongst friends and colleagues in scientific circles. A prayer found amongst his notes reads: "Almighty God, Who has created man in Thine own image, and made him a living soul that he might seek after Thee, and have dominion over Thy creatures, teach us to study the works of Thy hands, that we may subdue the earth to our use, and strengthen the reason for Thy service; so to receive Thy blessed word, that we may believe on Him whom Thou has sent, to give us knowledge of salvation and the remission of our sins. All of which we ask in the name of the same Jesus Christ, our Lord" [16].

These are only some of the outstanding great scientists who invented or discovered something worthwhile and found no conflict whatsoever between their faith in the Bible as the perfect word of God and their scientific genius.

There are many others like **Fleming**, the pioneer of electronics who wrote: "There is abundant evidence that the Bible, though written by men, is not the product of the human mind. By countless multitudes it has always been revered as a communication to us from the Creator of the Universe" [17]. **Lister** who invented antiseptic surgery declared: "I am a believer in the fundamental doctrines of Christianity" [18]. **Simpson** who invented anaesthetics, when asked about the greatest discovery he made in his life said: "That I found the Saviour" [19]. **Dalton** who established the atomic theory was a committed Christian. **The Wright brothers** who invented the powered aircraft both received Jesus Christ as their personal Saviour during their youth and refused to work on the Lord's Day even when the race for registering this invention was in a very critical stage. We must not forget great scientists like **Babbage** (computer science), **von Braun** (space rockets), **Euler** (calculus), **Mendel** (genetics), **Pascal** (probability), **Ramsay** (chemistry) ... and many others who proclaimed their uncompromising faith to the whole world [20].

These are some examples of some of the great scientists who believed that the Bible *is* the word of God the Creator. But such scientists are not all from bygone days when science was developing. Today also, there are many scientists recognised for their contributions in all fields of science who accept the inspiration and the literal interpretation of the Bible from Genesis to Revelation. They all agree that true science *always* confirms that the Bible is the perfect word of God.

REFERENCES

1. Tiner, J.H. *Johannes Kepler - Giant of Faith and Science*, Mott Media, Milford (Michigan), 1977, pp. 195-6.
2. ibid. inside front cover.
3. ibid. p. 178.
4. ibid. p. 197.
5. More, L.T. *The Life and Works of the Honourable Robert Boyle*, Oxford University Press, Oxford, 1944, p. 171.
6. Tiner, J.H. *Isaac Newton - Inventor, Scientist, and Teacher*, Mott Media, Milford (Michigan), 1975 - inside front cover.
7. ibid.
8. ibid.
9. Boreham, F.W. *A Handful of Stars: Tests that Moved Great Minds*, Epworth Press, London, 1933, p. 180.
10. Williams, E.L. and Mulfinger, G. *Physical Science for Christian Schools*, Bob Jones University Press, Greenville (South Carolina), 1974, p. 458.
11. Corbin, D.F.M. *A Life of Matthew Fontaine Maury*, USN & CSN, Sampson & Low & Co., 1888.
12. Crowther, J.G. *British Scientists of the Nineteenth Century*, Routledge & Kegan Paul, London, 1962, p. 138.
13. Tiner, J.H. *Louis Pasteur - Founder of Modern Medicine*, Mott Media, Michigan, (1990), p. 75.
14. Thomson, W. *Journal of the Victoria Institute*, Vol. 124, p. 267.
15. Morris, H.M. *Men of Science, Men of God*, Master Books, Colorado Springs, 1982, p. 66.
16. Williams and Mulfinger (Ref. 10), p. 487.
17. Watson, D.C.C. *Myths and Miracles - A New Approach to Genesis 1-11*, Creation Science Foundation, Acacia Ridge (Queensland, Australia), 1988, p. 113.
18. Morris (Ref. 15), p. 67.
19. Morris (Ref. 15), p. 52.
20. Lamont, A. *21 Great Scientists who Believed the Bible*, Creation Science Foundation, Brisbane, 1995.

PART II - CREATION OR EVOLUTION: DOES SCIENCE HAVE THE ANSWER?

Chapter 3
WHAT IS ALL THE FUSS ABOUT?

"For the time will come when they will not endure sound doctrine but after their own lusts shall they heap to themselves teachers, having itching ears; And they shall turn away their ears from the truth, and shall be turned unto fables" (2 Tim 4:3-4).

The time spoken of by the apostle Paul has now come - for never in the history of humanity have so many people been misled by so few. Never before has there been such a concerted effort to cheat people out of their logic and faith. Never before has Satan been able to occupy so many leading positions in universities and science laboratories around the world trying to deceive people with lies and to use those whom he deceives to brainwash students from a very early age.

The first recorded question in the Bible, "Hath God said?", was asked by Satan as he took the form of the serpent, the most subtle of all animals in the Garden of Eden (Gen 3:1). The aim of the question was to make Eve doubt the word of God. Within a very short time he managed to deceive half the world's population (Eve!), who in turn managed to obtain the support of her husband, the other half! How did Satan do it? By lying, questioning the word of God and instilling doubt in Eve's mind. Sadly Eve fell into the trap: she listened, doubted and disobeyed.

Satan's methods have not changed, although they seem more sophisticated to go with the age. Today he has achieved hundreds of

PhDs and, wearing the cap and gown, he chairs most science departments at the top universities of the world. He is still propagating the same lies with the same objective. All he needs to do is to make people doubt the word of God; non-believers will then have "science" as an excuse to stay away from the truth, while believers will spend precious years of their life unable to witness or enjoy the blessings of the Lord. Sadly, Satan has been succeeding: in schools, universities, "scientific" circles, and even in some christian fellowships, people are turning away from the truth because they have been brainwashed to believe in evolution.

In order to convince people to believe in such an unbelievable theory, the process of brainwashing has to start at a very early age when children do not question what the so-called scientists say!

Let us face the issue and not bury our heads in the sand. In almost every school, there are teachers who, having been deceived by Satan's lies at university, are determined to teach evolution as science and fact to our children and young people starting as early as when they are 4 or 5 years old. Those same teachers (who include in many cases teachers of Religious Education) have an aggressive attitude towards anyone who still believes the biblical account of Creation or Noah's ark. In my own experience, I have had long discussions with teachers who taught my children from the age of 5, that Noah's ark is a fairy tale and that no one who knows about science can believe in creation. True christian teachers are afraid to take a stand because they might lose their jobs. Those who *have* paid that price for taking the Lord's side are but few in number, and consider it a small price compared to what the Saviour did at the cross of Calvary. Non-christian teachers take an unreasonably aggressive attitude towards this subject, refusing to give any consideration to the scientific evidence presented to them.

In this section we are going to consider the very important issue of creation versus evolution. This subject touches the life of each and everyone of us, because it deals with origins: where did all this universe come from, with its sun and stars? Where did this planet Earth come from with all its plant life and animal life? And most important of all, the question we have asked so many times and got all sorts of contradictory answers: where did *we* come from?

Where did the human race originally come from? Were we the result of a big bang that happened billions of years ago followed by a series of accidents, when some dead, inorganic, inanimate substances decided to come together and form the first cell which gradually evolved until it became a human being?

Or are we the result of an act of a loving and caring Creator, who created us on the sixth day of His creation week several thousand years ago, created us in His own image to have fellowship with Him and to live with Him forever?

There are two main theories of origin. On one hand we have the General Theory of Organic Evolution put forward by Charles Darwin [1] and others in the past century, and updated to what is now known as Neo-Darwinism. It is the theory that all living things arose by a naturalistic, materialistic evolutionary process from a single source, which itself arose by a similar process from a dead, inanimate world. It is also known as the molecule-to-man theory.

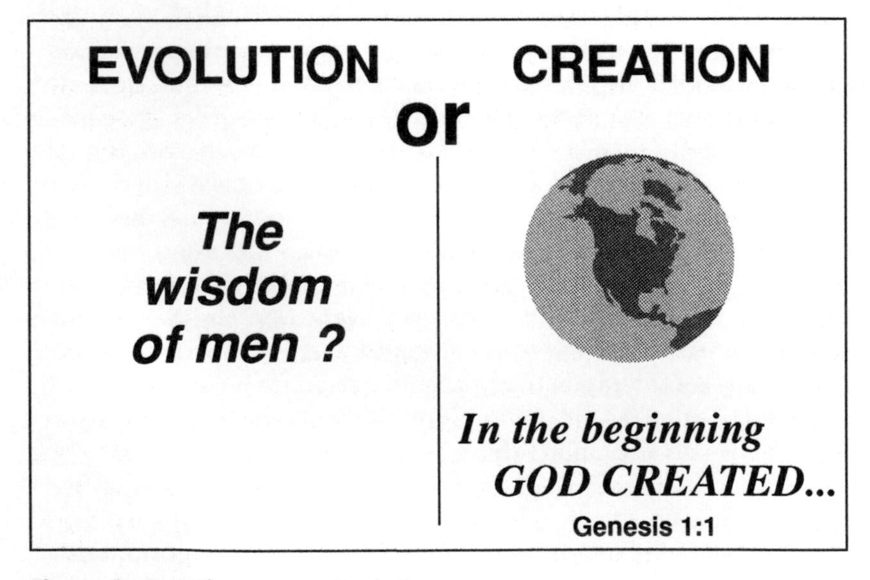

Figure 2: Creation versus Evolution

On the other hand we have the account of Creation (or the Creation model) as found in the book of Genesis [2], the first book of the Bible, written by Moses about 3500 years ago, and claiming to have been inspired by God. This account of Creation records that all basic animal and plant types were brought into existence by acts of God using special creative processes which are not operative today.

One can immediately see that, despite all attempts, the two cannot be reconciled. There is no place in evolution for a God who is interested in His creation and who sent His Son to die at the cross to save us from eternal death. Similarly there is no room for evolution if one accepts the authority and the divine inspiration of the Bible.

If one rejects the account of creation and the flood, all the basic moral and ethical principles must also be rejected. "But does it really matter?" some may ask. Of course it does! If we say that Genesis is not important, we are no longer taking the whole Bible seriously. After all, the New Testament alone has over 100 quotations from Genesis. The Lord Himself referred to Genesis in several instances. He declared very plainly, "For had ye believed Moses, ye would have believed me: for he wrote of me. But if ye believe not his writings, how shall ye believe my words?" (John 5:46-47). In Genesis we find the source of many christian beliefs and the basis for much christian doctrine: creation, good and evil, the origin of sin, the holiness of God, punishment of sin, death, the promise of a Saviour, marriage, and clothes, to mention but a few.

If God is the Creator and He is in control then He sets the rules. In Genesis God sets out the moral standards being trampled upon by evolutionists today. The basis of marriage, for example, "they shall be one flesh", is recorded in Genesis 2:24. The "two" are man and woman, "male and female created he them" (Gen 1:27), rejecting any justification for homosexuality which is totally accepted and justified by evolution. The teaching on both issues was confirmed by the Lord Jesus as recorded in the New Testament: "Have ye not read, that he which made them at the beginning made them male and female, And said, For this cause shall a man leave father and mother and shall cleave to his wife: and they twain shall be one flesh? Wherefore they are no more twain, but one flesh. What therefore God hath joined together, let not man put asunder" (Matt 19:4-6).

The sanctity of the human life is based on the fact that only God the Creator gives and takes life, thus setting the rules about abortion and euthanasia. All these issues are rejected by evolutionists on the basis that if humans are a product of chance they can set their own moral standards. If human beings are the product of survival of the fittest, then killing the unfit or the unborn is part of the process of evolution. If human beings descended from apes then abortion is like killing any other animal. The sanctity of human life is trodden under the feet of evolutionists with no remorse. Racism, fighting, manipulation and many other aspects have been justified by evolutionary philosophy: "Let us eat and drink; for to morrow we die" (1 Cor 15:32). The implications are manifold and we need to know the facts and take a stand - no compromise!

We are going to look at an extensive amount of evidence to help us choose between the two. I urge you to check every point carefully, verify and question and use your minds like you have never used them before. Believers, we have the mind of Christ which is a renewed mind, a penetrating mind, a discerning mind, a logical and sound mind (1 Cor 2:16). Let us use our minds to the limit!

Those who have not accepted the Lord Jesus, the Creator, as your own personal Saviour, I urge you to examine the evidence and be honest in your search for the truth.

REFERENCES

1. Darwin, C. *The Illustrated Origin of the Species*, (Abridged and introduced by Richard Leaky), Book Club Associates, London, 1979.
2. *The Holy Bible,* King James Version: Cambridge University Press, UK, 1981.

Chapter 4
BIG BANG OR BIG BELIEF?

"But God made the earth by his power" (Jer 10:12).

Majestically, the Bible opens with the words: "In the beginning, God created" (Gen 1:1). Evolutionists have come up with what they call science's answer to creation and the need for God: the Big Bang.

According to Cambridge Professor Stephen Hawking who publicised the Big Bang as science in his book *Brief History of Time* , the theory goes something like this:

In the beginning there was a 'cosmic egg' which was the size of a speck of dust on a table. This particle accommodated the condensed mass of the entire universe!

Where did this come from? It was there from the beginning! (People can accept Hawking's word but refuse to accept God's word!)

The theory then explains why the Big Bang occurred about ten thousand million years ago. It is because it takes about that long for intelligent people to evolve!!

Then an early generation of stars first had to form. These stars converted some of the original hydrogen and helium into elements like carbon and oxygen, out of which we are made [1], and so on.

Kraus in a recent book published in 1993 entitled *Has Hawking Erred?* [2], calculated a conservative estimate of the mass of the universe as 8×10^{25} tons. The conclusion of his book was: "The idea that a speck of matter smaller than a dust particle on my table could have accommodated the condensed mass of the entire universe, stretches credibility beyond its limits ... The Big Bang theory must be seriously questioned".

It is hardly surprising that in 1992 E.J. Lerner wrote a 465-page book entitled *The Big Bang Never Happened: A Startling Refutation of the Dominant Theory of the Origin of the Universe*. In his book he argues that the Big Bang is nothing but a myth which contradicts scientific observations:

"The Big Bang has flunked every test, yet it remains the dominant cosmology, and the tower of theoretical entities and hypotheses climbs steadily higher. Today's cosmologists have ... thus returned to a form of mathematical myth ... Entire careers in cosmology have now been built on theories which have never been subjected to observational test, or have failed such tests and been retained nonetheless.

"There is more than science involved here. While the Big Bang as a scientific theory is less and less supported by data, its prominence in our culture has increased. The scientific press has taken it as unquestionable truth" [3].

Lerner's proposed theory to replace the Big Bang is based on even wilder imagination, a trend amongst most evolutionary 'scientists' today!

Both Kraus and Lerner are not Christians.

In August 1989, the widely read British journal *Nature* ran a lead editorial entitled "Down with the Big Bang" [4], which described the theory as unacceptable and predicted that "it is unlikely to survive the decade ahead". The journal concluded about the Big Bang: "In all respects save that of convenience, this view of the origin of the universe is thoroughly unsatisfactory. It is an effect whose cause cannot be identified or even discussed".

The comments of Dr Colin Patterson, Senior Palaeontologist at the British Museum of Natural History in London, given in an interview on the BBC, (4 March 1982), describe the so-called evidence for Evolution as "little more than story telling"! [5].

The situation becomes worse when so-called scientists then believe the fairy tales they relate to people and set out to get the evidence at a great material cost to humanity, not to mention the greater moral and spiritual cost.

To illustrate this and the manipulation of data to promote Evolution at any cost, let me take you on a quick trip to Cape Canaveral, to the headquarters of the American Space Agency NASA, and in particular to the operation room dealing with the cosmic background explorer satellite (COBE).

In their attempt to make the Big Bang theory look scientific, evolutionists said that the fireballs - which, supposedly evolved into stars and galaxies - should appear as bumps on a map plotting the temperature differences of the background microwave radiation.

Put in simple terms: if scientists point their detectors out in different directions they should see slight differences in temperature of the microwaves. Instead of forming a straight horizontal line when plotted on a map of the sky, the results should show hills and valleys!

The logic was then turned upside down; if the bumps are there, then the Big Bang is true! In 1989, the Explorer satellite was launched to get this evidence.

1991 - the satellite was still reporting no bumps! According to Princeton University scientists reporting in the *New Scientist* magazine, under the heading "Background radiation deepens confusion for big bang theorists":

> "Many accepted theories of galaxy formation will have to go, if the data build-up from the cosmic background explorer satellite is published ... Big Bang theorists will be in a lot of trouble when the data is released" [6].
>
> The source went on to say: "But the authorities concerned are not releasing the data". I wonder why!

1992 - still no bumps! Panic in the operation room! Funding is in danger! Big Bang is in great trouble!

April 1992 - decision was taken to call all reporters and claim that the bumps were found. Reporters all over the world had a field day! Almost every single newspaper in the UK carried articles the next morning against God and creation.

No one was told that the team had to admit that the bumps were not real bumps, but were well within the level of instrumental noise. And no one was told that the bumps represented a difference in temperature of 1/100,000 of a degree - which is absolutely insignificant!

No one was told that even if there were bumps, there are so many scientific explanations for them other than the "Big Bang"! That was only revealed later on, under pressure, to scientific sources.

Lerner in his book *The Big Bang Never Happened* describes the reaction of the media:

"When the results were announced at an Astronomical Society meeting, there was actual cheering (not a common event at scientific conferences!). But after a few hours, theorists realised that this was actually bad news" [7].

If you are a Christian, do you feel threatened by such reports? Are you worried? Is your faith shaken? Do you panic or search for a compromise to *accommodate* the Big Bang in Genesis 1?

If you are not a Christian, do you feel betrayed that those scientists, whom you trust, do not tell you the truth, the whole truth and nothing but the truth? Do you feel angry that you put your trust in them concerning matters as important as your origin and hence, your destination, yet they betray your trust?

This is not the only problem with the Big Bang. We shall consider the verdict of the fundamental laws of science in the next chapter. But first let us look briefly at another embarrassment for the Big Bang supporters, referred to as the "age dilemma"!

Evolutionists believed that the stars are 25 billion years old (we shall consider the true ages in Chapter 9). In 1994, the Hubble Telescope, having been fitted with the most recent and sophisticated equipment gave readings for the age of the universe: 8-12 billion years! This was reported in *Time Magazine* Nov. 7, 1994 under the heading "Oops? ... Wrong Answer!" saying, "If the age appears to be more like 8 billion, then the Big Bang may be shot!" [8].

This went on as the data were analysed and in *Time Magazine* March 6, 1995, under the heading "Unravelling universe....Here's why Cosmology is in Chaos..." the reporter wrote "You can't be older than your ma! ... It seems the universe hasn't caught on to this bit of common-sense" [9]. The common sense here is the fact that one needs a universe to be existing before any star can be "formed" in it - yet the measurements showed stars older than the universe!

Stephen Hawking concludes his book: *Brief History of Time* by saying: "If we find the answer to that (why it is that we and the universe exist), it would be the ultimate triumph of human reason- for then we would know the mind of God" [10].

If people like Hawking are willing to search, they would have found the answer in the Bible. Paul writes to the Corinthians : "For who hath known the mind of the Lord", and gives them the answer in the same verse: "But we have the mind of Christ" (1 Cor 2:16).

We shall look at common-sense in the coming chapters, keeping in mind that those who promote such ridiculous theories in a desperate attempt by Satan to undermine the power of God, are "willingly ignorant" (2 Pet 3:5).

REFERENCES

1. Hawking, S. *A Brief History of Time*, Bantam Books, Great Britain, 1995.
2. Kraus, G. *Has Hawking Erred? A sceptical appraisal of his best-selling 'A Brief History of Time' - revealing a major scientific fallacy*, Janus Publishing Company, Great Britain, 1993, p. 153.
3. Lerner, E.J. *The Big Bang Never Happened: A Startling Refutation of the Dominant Theory of the Origin of the Universe*, Simon & Schuster Ltd, London, 1991, p. 54.
4. "Down with the Big Bang", Editorial, *Nature*, 10 August 1989.
5. "Cladistics", Dr Colin Patterson, BBC interview 4 March 1992.
6. Vaughan, C. "Background radiation deepens the confusion for Big Bang theorists", *New Scientist,* 28 April 1990, p. 38.
7. Lerner (Ref. 3) p. 31.
8. Lemonick, M.D. "Oops? ... Wrong Answer", *Time Magazine*, 7 November, 1994.
9. Lemonick, M.D. and Nash, J.M. "Unravelling Universe ... Here's why the Cosmology is in Chaos", *Time Magazine*, 6 March, 1995.
10. Hawking (Ref. 1) p. 193.

Chapter 5
SCIENCE SPEAKS

"If any of you lack wisdom, let him ask of God, that giveth to all men liberally and upbraideth not; and it shall be given him" (James 1:5).

"Come now, let us reason together, saith the LORD" (Isa 1:18).

Let us compare the Big Bang theory with Creation using some fundamental Laws of Science, and see which one contradicts these laws and which one is in harmony with them.

First, consider the Laws of Thermodynamics (for simplicity, "thermodynamics" comes from two Greek words meaning heat-power). All scientists are controlled by two basic laws as they research or experiment, and these are the two Laws of Thermodynamics. There are no exceptions to these laws. From the simplest experiment to the most complex, all processes in the universe must obey the Laws of Thermodynamics.

The First Law is known as **the Law of Conservation of Energy** and it states that energy is not being created or destroyed. Recently scientists discovered that matter could be *converted* to energy; however the sum total of matter and energy cannot be changed. This implies that the universe could not have created itself. If it had a beginning, the universe must have been created by a "cause" outside of itself using processes which are not operative today. Therefore, the Big Bang theory contradicts the First Law of Thermodynamics

Creation states that energy is not being created or destroyed, in complete harmony with the First Law. Creation goes a step further to explain why: energy is not being created because on the seventh day of the creation week, God stopped all creation work (Gen 2:2). Energy is not being destroyed either, because God is "upholding all things by the word of his power" (Heb 1:3).

The Second Law gives a more fascinating comparison. It states that all physical systems, left to themselves tend to become disordered and chaotic. Disorder is referred to in thermodynamics as "entropy" - as time goes on, entropy increases (for a detailed explanation of entropy see reference 1). In its most simple terms, entropy has been called **"Time's Arrow"**, and the arrow of time is always pointing downwards. Hence, given time, everything deteriorates, decays or dies. Now the Big Bang theory claims that this ordered universe came out of a chaotic explosion, thus contradicting the Second Law. It is worth noting at this point that not only the Big Bang, but the *whole* theory of Evolution contradicts the Second Law. Evolution says that there is a universal process of development and increasing order and complexity in the universe - with time things get better. We supposedly started with one cell and now we have a complex human being. Time's Arrow is pointing upwards in Evolution, completely contradicting the Second Law! This problem is acknowledged by a number of evolutionists. For example Jeremy Rifkin in *Entropy: A New World View,* writes:

"We believe that evolution somehow magically creates greater overall value and order on earth. Now that the environment we live in is becoming so dissipated and disordered that it is apparent to the naked eye, we are beginning for the first time to have second thoughts about our views on evolution, progress, and the creation of things of material value. ... Evolution means the creation of larger and larger islands of order at the expense of greater seas of disorder in the world. There is not a single biologist or physicist who can deny this central truth. Yet, who is willing to stand up in a classroom or before a public forum and admit it" [2].

According to Creation, when man sinned, God cursed the earth and subjected it to decay and death. The Bible records that "the whole creation groaneth and travaileth in pain together" (Rom 8:22). The Psalmist expresses the situation talking about the heavens and the earth : "Yea, all of them shall wax old like a garment" (Ps 102:26). Time's Arrow is pointing downwards in Creation, in complete harmony with the Second Law. So we have two basic universal laws of Science in complete contradiction to Evolution, but in complete harmony with Creation.

The Laws of Thermodynamics not only point back to a time when creation must have occurred, but they also point to a future time when

Time's Arrow hits rock-bottom! When the available energy eventually approaches zero, the ultimate heat death about which Peter warns us will come about: "the heavens shall pass away with a great noise, and the elements shall melt with fervent heat, the earth also and the works that are therein shall be burned up" (2 Pet 3:10).

Some evolutionists try to get out of this deadly trap by one of two ways: they either say that the Laws of Thermodynamics are not universal, that is scientists might come out with a test result that contradicts the Laws; or they resort to the "open system" argument saying that the laws do not hold for an open system where external energy can be pumped into the system.

The first argument that these two laws do not apply to the origin of the universe is overturned by the fact that science is based on observation. The two laws are known to be valid when applied to *all* mass-energy systems and processes in observable space and time. The Laws of Thermodynamics are science. A theory based on an unobserved, imaginary contradiction to millions of consistent experimental observations cannot be classified as science!

The argument about the open system is defeated by the **Third Law of Thermodynamics** which states that order is maximum at absolute

LAWS OF THERMODYNAMICS

- **1st LAW** ENERGY IS NEITHER BEING CREATED NOR DESTROYED
- **2nd LAW** ALL PHYSICAL SYSTEMS, WHEN LEFT TO THEMSELVES, WILL MOVE IN A DIRECTION FROM ORDER TO CHAOS
- **3rd LAW** ORDER IS MAXIMUM AT ABSOLUTE ZERO TEMPERATURE (-273°C) ADDING RAW ENERGY REDUCES ORDER

Figure 3: Thermodynamics

zero (-273 ^{0}C) because there the entropy is zero. This implies that adding raw heat energy to an open system will only increase the disorder. It will inevitably result in a decrease in functional information available in the order of that system. Without the presence of a directing program and a conversion mechanism (like chlorophyll in plants) raw energy from any source will increase disorder like a bull in a china shop! (For a detailed explanation of open systems see reference 3.)

The assumption that an explosion could produce order clearly contradicts the laws of science. A further assumption that this explosion resulted in a uniform radial expansion of energy and matter contradicts another scientific law - **the Principle of Conservation of Angular Momentum**. This principle states that uniform radial motion could never give rise to curvilinear motion. Hence the assumption that a linearly expanding gas converted into orbiting galaxies and planetary systems is just not possible according to yet another law of science.

Consider also the famous **Law of Cause and Effect**. This states that for every effect there must be a cause which is superior in every aspect, showing that the universe could not have created itself as the Big Bang theory assumes. The universe (effect) needed a cause which is outside it and is superior to it. The only "cause" that is outside space and time and is superior to all is the Creator, the one who could say "Before Abraham was, I am" (John 8:58), and challenge "Where wast thou when I laid the foundations of the earth?" (Job 38:4).

It is clear from the above that the Big Bang is the attempt of false science to provide an alternative to Creation. But as we are lost in the wonder of this vast universe we cannot but praise the great Creator: "The heavens declare the glory of God; and the firmament sheweth his handywork" (Ps 19:1).

REFERENCES

1. Morris, H.M. and Parker, G.E. *What is Creation Science?* (revised ed.), Master Books, El Cajon, California, 1987, pp. 190-205.
2. Rifkin, J. *Entropy: A New World View,* Viking Press, New York, 1980, p. 55.
3. Morris (Ref. 1) pp. 205-220.

Chapter 6
IS LIFE A MIRACLE OR DID IT JUST HAPPEN?

"And the LORD God formed man of the dust of the ground, and breathed into his nostrils the breath of life; and man became a living soul" (Gen 2:7).

Now let us go back to the very beginning - how did it all start? According to Evolution, several billion years ago, at one spot on Earth, some dead inorganic substances decided of their own will, and with no external forces except the existing natural phenomena, to come together and form the first living cell.

The first point in this theory is the assumption that life could come from dead matter. This was the general belief in the days of Darwin. People believed in spontaneous generation. They believed that dead meat generates maggots, and rubbish generates mice, flies and insects. Louis Pasteur then proved that all this was wrong, and established the **Law of Biogenesis** which states that "Life can only come from life". Even after experimental evidence proved that spontaneous generation is not scientific [1], scientists still cling to the idea of the spontaneous generation of microscopic animals. To disprove this, Pasteur boiled some broth to kill any microbes. Using special glass apparatus, he allowed air to circulate over the broth, preventing microbes in the air from reaching the broth. Pasteur's work showed that microbes appeared in the broth only if they were allowed in with the air. Needless to say, Pasteur was a strong opponent of Darwin's theory. Hence evolution contradicts another famous scientific law - Pasteur's Law of Biogenesis, by assuming that the first living cell came from dead matter. With Creation there is no problem, for a living God gave life to all living things.

Once again evolutionists argue that this law is an extrapolation of experimental results as carried out by Pasteur, and hence it may not hold under all conditions. However, the whole field of microbiology is based on the fact that even in microbes, life comes only from life. The law *is* a universal law. One cannot imagine the chaos in the medical field if this law suddenly ceases to be universal and microbes start coming from non-living matter!

In the days of Darwin, it was thought that the simple cell was really simple. Today modern science tells us that the simple cell contains thousands of different kinds of proteins and other substances, with billions of each kind along with all kinds of DNA, RNA and other highly complex molecules arranged in an incredibly complicated system - all this is one "simple" cell!

The more scientists carry out research about DNA and the genes, the more they are fascinated by the complexity of life. For the purpose of our subject, I shall try to simplify the situation in order to give the reader an idea of the implication of the complexity of this subject on the theory of Evolution. The subject is tackled in greater detail by Christians who have specialised in this fascinating field. I recommend the book: *What is Creation Science?* [2] for further study.

The two basic parts of every living system are DNA and protein. All human characteristics are "spelled out" in about two metres of DNA all coiled up when life starts off as a tiny little ball the size of a small dot on this page!

DNA is built like a string of pearls, whose links act like letters of the alphabet to spell out hereditary instructions. Proteins are chains of amino acids. Each chain coils into a special shape that has a special function like muscle contraction, digestion, etc. For example, chains of several hundred DNA bases tell the cell how to make a protein called haemoglobin, and that protein functions as the oxygen carrier in red blood cells.

The start of the relationship between DNA and protein causes a major problem to evolutionists. Left to themselves, the natural trend of acid-base reactions is to scramble up DNA and protein units in all sorts of deadly combinations. This is why, even under sophisticated and controlled laboratory conditions, the famous experiments carried out by Miller, Fox and others to produce life in the laboratory never worked [3]. Left to time, chance, and their inherent chemical properties, the bases and amino acids of DNA and proteins would react in ways that would destroy any hope of producing life.

To make a living cell alive scientists need *Creation*! Only creation could organise matter into the first living cells. Once the parts are in place, there is nothing mysterious in the way cells make proteins. It is what we know and can explain about DNA and protein and the laws of chemistry which point out that life is a result of creation.

Dr Michael Denton, an authority on molecular biology who is not (yet) a Creationist, in his book *Evolution: A Theory in Crisis* refers to the chemical evolution of life as "simply an affront to reason". He goes on to say :

"The really significant finding that comes to light from comparing the proteins' amino acid sequences is that it is impossible to arrange them in any sort of an evolutionary series" [4].

Lipson, the British physicist comments in an article published by *Physics Bulletin* May 1980 entitled "A Physicist Looks at Evolution":

"If living matter is not, then, caused by the interplay of atoms, natural forces, and radiation, how has it come into being?" [5].

After dismissing a sort of directed evolution, he concludes:

"I think, however, that we must go further than this and admit that the only acceptable explanation is creation ... I know this is anathema to physicists, as indeed it is to me ... but we must not reject a theory that we do not like if the experimental evidence supports it".

Hence the conclusion from the modern sciences of molecular biology, genetics and physics is that life is a miracle performed by the Creator.

Mathematically speaking, the possibility of such a simple cell coming about by chance (assuming it is possible to obtain it from dead matter), has been calculated by a number of mathematicians. One of the more optimistic information scientists, M. Golay, calculated the probability of the accidental ordering of particles into a replicating system. He calculated the figure based on the assumption that it was accomplished by a series of 1500 successive events, each with the generously high probability of 1/2. The probability would have been much lower if it had to be accomplished in a single chance event. The result was 1 in 10^{450} , in other words 1 outcome in 10 raised to the power of 450 attempts!

To understand this number let us consider the total number of possible events in time and space. For the sake of argument let us take the evolutionary time scale of 3 trillion years (10^{20} seconds), and the total available space of 5 billion light years radius is equivalent to 10^{130} electrons. (One light year is the distance light travels in one year at a speed of 299,800 km per second.) If each particle can take part in one hundred billion billion (10^{20}) events *per second* then the greatest conceivable number of events that could have taken place in all of space and time would be: $10^{130} \times 10^{20} \times 10^{20} = 10^{170}$ events. When the probability of occurrence of an event (in this case 1 in 10^{450}) is smaller than one out of the number of events that could *ever possibly occur* (10^{170}) then the probability of its occurrence is considered by mathematicians to be zero.

Sir Fred Hoyle, the famous evolutionary Professor of Astronomy at Cambridge, spent time working out the possibility of life arising by chance. He made news under the heading "There must be a God" in the *London Daily Express* of 14 August 1981. This was the very conclusion he reached after detailed mathematical analysis of the belief that life could result from time, chance and the properties of matter. It was, according to Sir Fred Hoyle, comparable to the belief that "... a tornado sweeping through a junk-yard might assemble a Boeing 747 from the materials therein" [6].

We read in newspapers and hear reports claiming that scientists have been able to create life in their laboratories. Do not believe those reports, but examine them, looking carefully at the processes used and you will find out that scientists have not come anywhere near to creation of life or even the simplest form of cells. In some cases they used chemicals and applied a sophisticated source of energy that could not have existed in an early world. Even with such unrealistic systems, only certain chemicals were synthesised, which is a logical result, but nowhere near to the cell and certainly not living.

All those teams of PhDs and great specialised scientists; all the funds for research work; all the modern machinery, equipment and computers of the most sophisticated laboratories in the world, and scientists are not able to create the simple cell from dead matter. Yet evolutionists want us to believe that it simply happened on its own

Figure 4: Life is a Miracle

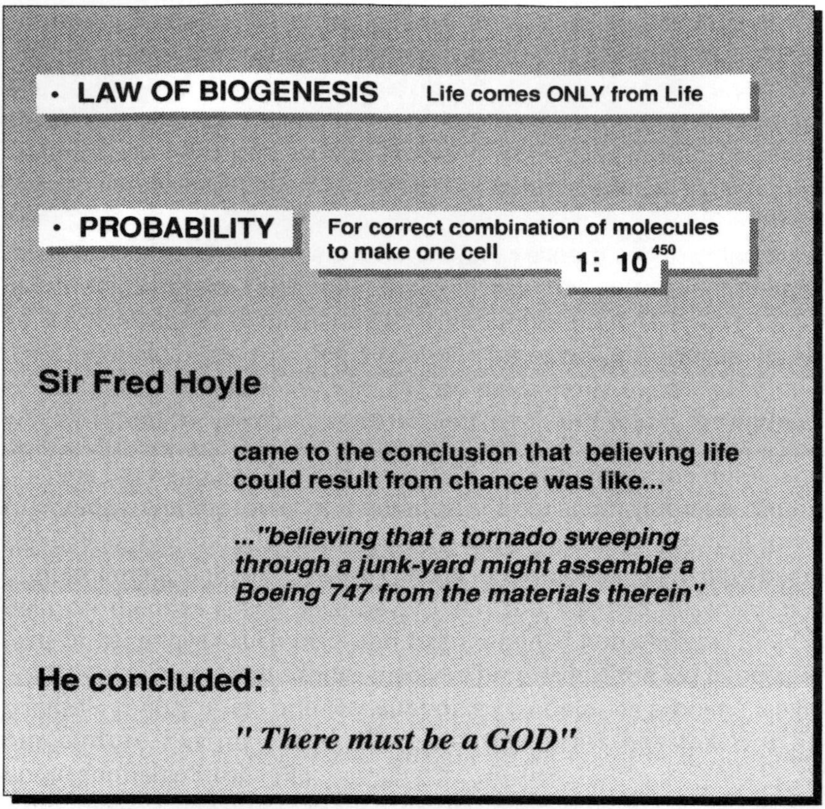

• LAW OF BIOGENESIS Life comes ONLY from Life

• PROBABILITY For correct combination of molecules to make one cell **$1: 10^{450}$**

Sir Fred Hoyle

came to the conclusion that believing life could result from chance was like...

..."believing that a tornado sweeping through a junk-yard might assemble a Boeing 747 from the materials therein"

He concluded:

" There must be a GOD"

billions of years ago assuming that by going back to the dark past, no one will be able to question them; but the facts are as clear as daylight.

Therefore, neither scientifically, nor mathematically, nor logically could the first cell have appeared by accident. More than faith would be necessary to believe in such an accident which evolutionists call science.

REFERENCES

1. Lamont, A. *21 Great Scientists Who Believed The Bible,* Creation Science Foundation, Brisbane, 1995, p. 148.
2. Morris, H.M. and Parker, G.E. *What is Creation Science?* (revised ed.), Master Books, El Cajon, California, 1987.
3. ibid. p. 39.
4. Denton, M. *Evolution: A Theory in Crisis*, Adler and Adler, Bethesda Maryland, 1985, p. 289.
5. Lipson, H.S. "A Physicist Looks at Evolution", *Physics Bulletin*, May 1980, p. 138.
6. Hoyle, Sir F. as quoted in "There must be a God", *Daily Express*, 14 August 1981.

Chapter 7
MUTATIONS - THE MIRACLE MAKERS

"For by him were ***all*** things created, that are in heaven, and that are in earth, visible and invisible" (Col 1:16).

Let us now move on a step further. How did the simple cell become a complicated human being? According to Evolution, it happened by a series of micro-mutations. Mutations are sudden changes in genetic structure brought about by external factors, like radiation, penetrating the germ cell. When these mutations are beneficial or helpful, they are supposedly preserved and passed on to the following generations and these are then responsible for developing a new superior kind.

Mutations should be distinguished from "natural selection", these expressions being used interchangeably to mislead people. The famous peppered moth example is often cited as evidence for evolution, when in fact it is only evidence for natural selection! In the 1850s the light form of the peppered moth made up 98% of the moth population in England. They were well camouflaged on the light tree background, whereas the dark ones stood out and were spotted by birds who ate them. Then pollution due to the industrial revolution killed the lichen on the trees, revealing the dark colour of the bark. As a result, the dark moths were more camouflaged than the light ones. Thus the dark ones now had a better chance of survival resulting in 98% being dark moths in the 1950s. The moths themselves never changed. There were always dark and light moths. Although textbooks cite this as an example of "evolution going on today", it definitely is not!

Several examples can be cited about the amazing fit of organisms to their environment. When an adaptation involves a whole group of traits working together, with none of the individual pieces having any survival value until the whole set is functioning together, then evolutionists have a big problem. Famous examples are the Flicker woodpecker and the Bombardier beetle[1].

The woodpecker is continually banging its beak into trees. To do this and survive it must have a thick skull, with shock-absorbing tissues, muscles and other parts. It also requires a very long tongue to reach under the tree bark! All these traits must be fully developed together for the woodpecker to survive.

The Bombardier beetle has an igneous chemical defence mechanism. When an attacker comes to eat the beetle, the beetle turns round and blasts the attacker in the face with hot noxious gases at 100 ^{0}C, which allows the beetle to escape! To achieve the firing with success, the beetle has to mix the right amount of two chemicals: hydrogen peroxide and hydroquinones, making use of two enzymes and enzyme blockers, pressure tanks, and a whole series of nerve and muscle attachments for aim and control.

Imagine for a moment that evolution is true. The attacker comes and the beetle mixes the wrong amounts and boom! it blows itself up! Wait several million years for the next beetle to evolve ... and so on! When it comes to adaptations that require several traits all depending on one another, time and chance, natural selection, or survival of the fittest have no hope. The only logical explanation is design and Creation.

Darwin analysed many features of animals and attributed them to survival of the fittest. He assumed that new traits, for example the long neck of the giraffe, were acquired characteristics due to the environment, and believed that these could be inherited. Giraffes supposedly got long necks because their ancestors stretched them to reach leaves high in the trees, then passed on more neck "pangenes" [2] to their offspring. This idea of progress through effort, which contributed to the early popularity of evolution, has since been proved wrong and discarded! Scientists know today what Darwin didn't know about heredity - that traits which are acquired through "effort" *cannot* be passed on to offspring.

As scientists discovered the errors in Darwin's assumptions they tried to develop Darwinism into a new form, *Neo*-Darwinism. They replaced this concept of use and disuse by the random changes in genes called mutations.

What does science have to say about mutations? All observed

natural mutations are ultimately either harmful or deadly, with *no exception*. Yet evolutionists claim (with no basis) that one in 10,000 mutations might not be harmful and they base the theory on this assumption.

Thousands of mutations were carried on the fruit fly. The results? Some blind, some without legs, some with short wings, but always inferior in the long run and less fit to survive. They also remained fruit flies.

Once again, mathematical probability quantifies the problem evolutionists have in assuming mutations are the mechanism of evolution. Mutations are rare, they occur on average perhaps once in every ten million duplications of a DNA molecule (1 in 10^7). The problem comes when one needs a *series* of related mutations; the odds of getting only two related mutations is $10^7 \times 10^7 = 10^{14}$, or one in one hundred trillion. Only four related mutations have a chance of one in 10^{28}, and the earth is not big enough to hold enough organisms to make this likely! Surprisingly, it was Huxley, the famous evolutionist, who worked out the probability of the evolution of the horse as 1 in $10^{3,000,000}$. As we saw in the previous chapter, the total number of possible events is only 10^{170} ! No wonder Denton writes :

"If complex computer programs cannot be changed by random mechanisms, then surely the same must apply to the genetic programmes (sic) of living organisms. The fact that systems in every way analogous to living organisms cannot undergo evolution by pure trial and error (i.e. mutation and selection) and that their functional distribution invariably conforms to an improbable discontinuum comes, in my opinion, very close to a formal disproof of the whole Darwinian paradigm of nature. By what strange capacity do living organisms defy the laws of chance which are apparently obeyed by all analogous complex systems?" [3].

Another major problem with mutations is that they are going the wrong way for evolution. They can never be used to explain build-up of genetic order as evolutionists claim. Mutations are errors in information and they will never result in an *overall* improvement to the original situation. Mutations are used by creationists to explain the breakdown of existing genetic order as a result of man's sin.

The only example of a beneficial mutation cited by evolutionists is sickle-cell anaemia, a disease of red blood cells. However, it is classified as beneficial only because the carrier of this cell becomes immune to malaria. This is because the life-span of the defective blood cell is shorter than the incubation period of the malaria. It is not due to any improvement in the blood cell [4]. So *only* in regions of the world where malaria is a common cause of death, carriers of sickle-cell anaemia are at an advantage. However, where the defective gene is inherited from both parents, the person usually dies before reaching adulthood. Hence sickle-cell anaemia is a harmful mutation after all!

Therefore, all the evidence points to the fact that mutations cannot be justified as the means of evolution. Mutations point to creation. They are changes occurring in already existing genes and all you get as a result of a mutation is a varied form of an already existing gene: variation within the type (after its kind!). In the next section we shall discuss the perfect environment that God created for man before sin entered the world. At this stage it is enough to point out that Adam and Eve were created perfect. The Bible tells us that after God created man on the sixth day He declared that everything "was very good" (Gen 1:31). Adam and Eve had no bad genes, but after they sinned the whole world came under the curse of God. Disease, pain, suffering and death entered the world. One of the effects of the curse was the bad genes caused by mutations. This has been increasing as time goes on pointing to the fact that the end of all things is near. Today geneticists estimate about 2000 genetic diseases are caused by mutation. Many of those who spent years in research can testify that all such mutations are bad [5].

As children we were told a fairy tale about a frog that changed into a prince. Today, evolutionists want us to believe that given 300 million years a frog really turns into a prince. Suddenly the fairy tale turns into science. The problem is that with so much science fiction going around today, people cannot draw the line between fact and fiction and the evolutionists exploit this situation. So we see that mutation, the proposed mechanism of Evolution, is in fact one further evidence against the theory of Evolution.

EVOLUTION BASED ON BENEFICIAL MUTATION

GENETIC SCIENTISTS:
Natural mutations are always harmful or deadly !

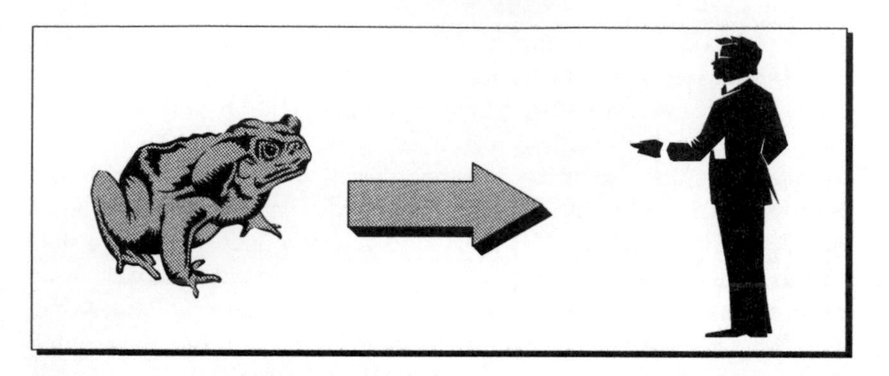

Figure 5: What about Mutations?

REFERENCES

1. Gish, D. *The Amazing Story of Creation*, Institute for Creation Research, CA, USA, 1990, pp. 96-102.
2. Ridley, M. *A Darwin Selection*, Fontana Press, London, 1994, p. 138.
3. Denton, M. *Evolution: A Theory in Crisis*, Adler and Adler, Bethesda Maryland, 1985, p. 315.
4. Rosevear, D. *Creation Science*, New Wine Press, England, 1991, p. 64.
5. Gish (Ref. 1) p. 42.

Chapter 8

THE FOSSILS SPEAK!

"Or speak to the earth, and it shall teach thee: and the fishes of the sea shall declare unto thee. Who knoweth not in all these that the hand of the LORD hath wrought this?" (Job 12:8-9).

When I study the fossil record, the only so-called material evidence for evolution, I am reminded of the words of our Lord Jesus Christ to the Pharisees when they asked Him to rebuke the disciples because they were rejoicing and praising God: "... if these should hold their peace, the stones would immediately cry out" (Luke 19:40).

Today many Christians are exposed to the fossil record by so-called scientists, and they feel that their faith is threatened by such evidence, as they assume that it supports evolution. Consequently, they "hold their peace" and stop rejoicing and praising Jesus Christ, their Saviour and Creator. For the many Christians holding their peace, let me assure you that the stones, indeed the fossils in the stones are crying out loud and clear ***Creation!***

What are fossils? When an organism is trapped and swept away by running water, it is buried at some point by sediment. The sediment becomes compacted into rock and the organisms or their imprints become part of the rock. These are called fossils, and they are found all over the world.

To start with, any person examining this subject with an open mind must conclude that fossils are evidence of sudden death and quick burial, and not slow gradual death and decay. It is evidence of catastrophism not uniformitarianism. The graveyards of fossils all over the world are "living" evidence of the Biblical account of the universal flood in the days of Noah, as described in the book of Genesis.

If the fossil record favours evolution, we would expect, first of all, to find the oldest layers of rock having the most primitive forms of life, and gradually as we go up the different strata we expect to find more and more complex forms of life.

Do we find this? Not at all! There are *no* indisputable fossils below the Cambrian strata. Then, all of a sudden, fossils of billions of animals that are complex, like trilobites, jelly fish and worms, appear in the Cambrian strata. Even if we accept micro fossils of single cells, there is a gap with no fossils at all which, according to evolution, took 1.5 billion years. So in this aspect the fossil record is not in favour of evolution.

According to Creation all living things were created together, so their fossils appear together as the record shows. Running water usually groups all similar weights and dumps them together, which is why fossils are sorted according to size.

If the fossil record favours evolution, then we would also expect new basic types not to appear suddenly, but to possess some characteristics of their ancestral groups. So if fish gave rise to amphibians over 50 million years according to evolution, there must be millions of fossils showing transitional forms, that is fossils with part fins and part legs, or half fish and half amphibian. If reptiles gave rise to birds over millions of years, then we must find fossils with part forelimbs and part wings, or half reptile and half bird.

But in all the fossil record comprising of millions of fossils, not a single transitional form is to be found. Evolutionists cannot blame the size of the record, as Darwin hinted, for the absence of those forms. According to Newell, an evolutionist: "Many discontinuities tend to be more and more emphasised with increased collecting" [1]. Simpson, one of the world's foremost evolutionists wrote: "Regular absence of transitional forms is not confined to mammals, but is almost a universal phenomenon. It is possible to claim that such transitions are not recorded because they did not exist" [2].

Evolutionists cite a now-extinct animal called Archaeopteryx as an example of a transitional form between reptiles and birds. In fact Archaeopteryx was a **bird:** it had perching feet, the wings of a bird, feathers identical to modern bird feathers, a bird-like skull and a 'wishbone'. Above all that, it *flew*! The fact that it had claws on its wings does not make it a transitional form. There are at least three birds living today that have claws on their wings: the Hoatzin in South America, the Touraco in Africa, and the Ostrich - and none of these are intermediates!!

The fact that Archaeopteryx had teeth also does not make it an intermediate. Some ancient birds had teeth and some did not. Some fishes have teeth and some amphibians and reptiles have teeth, but there are fishes and amphibians and reptiles with no teeth.

Recently fossils of a bird found in Texas were dated by evolutionists as 75 million years before Archaeopteryx. Yet evolutionists still hold onto Archaeopteryx in a desperate attempt to rescue the theory of Evolution.

Denton writes the following as a conclusion to the subject of transitional forms:

"In a very real sense, therefore, advocacy of the doctrine of continuity (e.g. evolutionism) has always necessitated a retreat from pure empiricism (i.e. logic and observation), and contrary to what is widely assumed by evolutionary biologists today, it has always been the anti-evolutionists (e.g. creationists), not the evolutionists, in the scientific community who have stuck rigidly to the facts and adhered to a more strictly empirical approach ... It was Darwin the evolutionist who was retreating from the facts" [3].

Could the fossil record be so cruel to evolution or is it that even the fossils cry out ***Creation!***

There are many aspects of the fossil record that cannot be explained by evolution. Some of these very briefly are:

1. **Polystrate fossils:** These are fossils standing in a vertical position instead of the usual horizontal, and spanning more than one layer of 6 metres (20 ft) thickness. Outstanding examples are fossils trees 24 metres (80 ft) high standing vertically or sometimes upside down and spanning 4-5 layers [4]. Each layer according to evolution must have taken millions of years to be deposited and there is no way evolutionists can explain how such fossilized trees remained upright while the layers were being deposited.
2. **Fossilized tracks of man and dinosaur:** These appear together in the Paluxy River basin in Texas [5]. According to evolution, dinosaurs are supposed to have become extinct 70 million years before man arrived on the scene. But here we have evidence that they roamed the world together, wiping out 70 million years of evolution. There

have been attempts by evolutionists to discredit this finding because of its significance, by claiming that the evidence has been tampered with. However, many scientists who saw the evidence say that such claims cannot be justified. Some of those footprints were tested and analysed in advanced laboratories. A section was cut through them and the pressure lines were clearly traced to the underlying layer [6]. If the footprints had been carved by forgers as claimed, there would have been no pressure lines going deep down the layer.

3. **Frozen mammoths in Siberia:** Found with their meals still in their stomachs, these show sudden death by freezing. According to evolution the freezing came very slowly over a long period of time. Hence there is no way evolution can explain this sudden freezing of mammoths. Some evolutionists went so far as to claim that all those mammoths ate a meal and jumped into a frozen river! It must have been a strange sort of Olympic games in Siberia that year!
4. **Pollen and spores from land plants in Cambrian strata:** According to evolution, when Cambrian strata were being deposited, land plants had not yet appeared on the scene and there is no way to explain the presence of pollen and spores in Cambrian rocks.
5. **The geologic column:** Described by geologists as a regular succession of rock layers starting with the oldest at the bottom and the youngest at the top, the geologic column is nowhere found complete and is not always as predicted. Vast areas of older rocks are found on top of younger ones - so huge and laid down so smoothly that they cannot be explained away as geologic faults.

These are just some of the aspects of the fossil record that can not be explained by evolution. But how do they fit in with Creation?

According to Creation, God created all the basic kinds of living things. Therefore we do not expect transitional forms and this is exactly what is shown by the fossil record.

The Bible account includes a catastrophic deluge or flood in the days of Noah as recorded in the book of Genesis. This explains scientifically the quick formation of sedimentary layers, it explains the presence of graveyards of fossils which required sudden death and quick burial. The flood also explains the existence of polystrate, vertical fossils as being due to the actions of tidal waves, volcanoes and excessive water pressures during the first forty days of the flood as recorded in the Bible. It explains the sudden change of climate and freezing of animals in Siberia and other areas after the vapour canopy, which provided a green-house effect over the whole world before the flood, emptied all its water on the earth during the flood. Consequently, the universal temperate climate ceased to exist giving rise to extreme climates. (See Section III.)

The Creation account provides scientific logical answers to all those problems where evolution fails to do so. Hence we see once again that the fossil record, the only so-called evidence for evolution, is not in favour of evolution but rather favours Creation.

To conclude, we are bombarded with fossils as evidence of evolution by teachers, professors, textbooks, museums, articles in "respectable" science magazines, and educational programs on radio and television. It is good to be aware of the truth and to know that the amount of scientific evidence in support of the claims of evolutionists is negligible. As a certain professor once said: "It is unbelievable how many unbelievable things an unbeliever has to believe in to be called an unbeliever"!

Evolution is Satan's modern tool to keep people away from God. As believers we have to be well armed with the word of God and be able to use it not only to defend ourselves against Satan's attacks, but also to be able to attack the enemy and snatch precious souls from his hands. Let us remember that: "... in all these things we are more than conquerors through him that loved us" (Rom 8:37).

REFERENCES

1. Newell, N.E. *Proc. Amer. Phil. Soc.* April 1959, p. 267.
2. Simpson, G.G. *Tempo and Mode in Evolution,* Columbia University Press, New York, 1944, p. 107.
3. Denton, Michael *Evolution: A Theory in Crisis*, Adler and Adler, Bethesda Maryland, 1985, p. 353-354.

4. Morris, H.M. *The Biblical Basis for Modern Science,* Baker Book House, Michigan, 1993, p. 325.
5. Baugh, C.E. and Wilson, C.A. *Dinosaur*, Promise Publishing Co., CA, 1987.
6. Ibid., photos & illustrations at centre of book.

Chapter 9
IS THE EARTH OLD OR YOUNG AND TIRED ?

"God himself that formed the earth and made it; he hath established it, he created it not in vain, he formed it to be inhabited" (Isa 45:18).

If asked for an estimate of the age of the earth, any believer or Bible scholar in the past century would have given a figure under 10,000 years without much hesitation. If asked the same question today, most Christians would give figures varying between thousands and billions of years. The responsibility for this confusion lies mainly with the theory of Evolution and a diminishing trust in the authority of the word of God.

As far as Christians are concerned, there is no need to worry or panic. The Bible is the perfect word of God, and evolutionists have nothing to base their dates on except the fact that they desperately need the billions of years to give evolution a chance to occur!

The dates we hear about everyday come from the radiometric-dating methods. Such methods have scientific problems and are based on assumptions which are altered to suit the evolutionary thinking and time scale required by the theory.

The Bible clearly tells us that there was no death before Adam sinned. Consequently there is no way that Christians can compromise and place billions of years between Gen 1:1 and 1:2. Such an idea was thought of as a panic solution by Christians who thought that the theory of Evolution was based on scientific facts. However, the word of God states that when God finished His creation work He proclaimed that *everything* was very good. Death and decay came about after creation was complete. Therefore the believer cannot accept fossils dated before this creation work and so more than 10,000 years old.

We cannot read stories to our children about dinosaurs who supposedly died out 70 million years before man arrived on the scene and then expect them to believe the Bible which teaches that God created man and dinosaur on the same day. We must treat this subject very seriously because we would be responsible before the Lord for misleading precious young souls if we attempted to compromise with evolution.

The compromise becomes even more impossible when we find out from Genesis that God created the sun and the stars on the fourth day, making them younger than the earth. Evolutionists require the sun to be there first in order to start the ball rolling. God decides the order of His creation: "...answer thou me. Where wast thou when I laid the foundations of the earth? Declare, if thou hast understanding" (Job 38:3-4).

It is from this standpoint that we shall look at the scientific evidence for a young earth so that we can have the answers to all those who ask us about our faith because "faith cometh by hearing, and hearing by the word of God" (Rom 10:17).

According to evolution the earth is very old. Their latest estimate for the age of the earth is 4.5 billion years. The most widely used dating methods are the radiometric-dating methods. For older rocks the uranium-thorium-lead and potassium-argon systems are used. For younger samples like archeological artifacts, the carbon-14 dating method is used.

The basis of these methods is that some elements are radioactive and with time they decay into other elements: uranium decays into thorium and thorium into lead. So taking a sample of a certain rock, scientists measure how much lead it contains and, knowing the rate of decay of uranium, the age of this rock is calculated.

There are several assumptions involved in the process:

- First, it is assumed that the rate of decay has always been constant but modern research shows that it is not. In most cases decay occurs rapidly at first and slows down later. A number of factors might have changed the rate of decay over the past thousands of years. One such important factor could have been a traumatic environmental change in the past such as the catastrophic flood in the days of Noah.
- Second, it is assumed that the initial quantity of the parent element (the first element in the chain) is known, but it is not; this is mainly guesswork. We do not know how much of the original rock was

uranium for example, and how much lead was already present initially.

- Third, it is assumed that the system under study is an isolated system. This means that the lead in our example came only from the uranium and this gives the very big age. Dr Melvin Cook, a Nobel award winner for his research in this field, found out that the lead does not come from uranium only, as assumed, and he applied a neutron reaction *correction* to the dating methods. A Cambrian Rock dated at 600 million years, gave a figure of several thousand years when this correction was applied to the method [1].

Even with all the assumptions in place, radiometric dating methods applied to the same rock have given answers varying by hundreds of millions of years. Evolutionists pick and choose the figures that fit with their preconceived idea about the age of the rock in question. This has been pointed out by a number of evolutionists like W. Stansfield who wrote:

"It is obvious that radiometric methods may not be the reliable dating methods they are often claimed to be. Age estimates on a given geological stratum using different methods are often quite different ... There is no absolutely reliable long term radiological clock". [2].

Recent research work carried out by Dr S. Austen on the Grand Canyon lava was presented in October 1992 at a meeting of the Geological Society of America. Austen showed that recent lava flows have a systematic variation in isotope ratios which has been *ignored* in the radiometric dating methods used. Such variations, if ignored, would have resulted in the indicated age of billions of years! [3]

The potassium-argon method is well known for its inconsistent results. It is enough to mention that when this method was applied to volcanic rocks known to be 200 years old from the historical record, it gave a range of values from 22 million years to 200 million years. So we can see that the millions that evolutionists speak about, and want people to take for granted, are just not true.

The famous carbon-14 dating method has one further assumption over and above those mentioned for other radiometric dating methods. It is that carbon-14 has already reached a state of equilibrium. In other words, it is assumed that the rate of production of carbon-14 is equal to its rate of decay. For such a state to be achieved, it requires 30,000 years from the start of the atmosphere, and since evolutionists talk about billions of years, they assume the equilibrium state has already been achieved. But modern studies (even by Dr. Libby [4] who discovered the method), show that the equilibrium state has not been achieved and that the formation is still at least *24% more* than decay [5]. Two important effects of this result can be highlighted briefly:

- First, all dates arrived at by this method now require adjustment, and such adjustments have reduced the dates dramatically. Several examples were recorded in the journal *Radiocarbon*, such as coal from Russia, supposedly 300 million years old, dated again at 1,680 years! [6]
- Second, from the equilibrium state measurements, scientists were able to calculate an approximate upper limit to the age of the atmosphere, and this was found to be a maximum of 10,000 years. Since we cannot imagine an earth without an atmosphere, the age of the earth has an upper limit of 10,000 in conformity with what God has revealed about creation.

It is also interesting to mention that a group of scientists in the USA dated the shell of a living snail using the carbon-14 dating method. The result was that the *living* snail was 27,000 years old![7]

In an article appearing in the *Anthropological Journal of Canada,* under the heading "Radiocarbon, Ages in Error", Robert Lee sets forth the truth of the matter:

"The troubles of the radiocarbon dating method are undeniably deep and serious ... it should be no surprise, then, that fully half of the dates are rejected. The wonder is, surely, that the remaining half come to be *accepted*." [8].

At a symposium on prehistory, Professor Brew summarised a common attitude among archaeologists towards the C14 dating method:

"If a C14 date supports our theories, we put it in the main text. If it does not entirely contradict them, we put it in a footnote. And if it is completely out of date, we just drop it" [9].

Dr John Eddy, an astro-geophysicist, in a report published in the *Geotimes* of September 1978 makes this comment:

"There is no evidence based solely on solar observations, Eddy stated, that the sun is 4.5 - 5 x 10^9 years old. 'I suspect', he said, 'that the sun *is* 4.5 billion years old. However, given some new and unexpected results to the contrary, and some time for frantic recalculation and theoretical readjustment, I suspect that we could live with Bishop Ussher's value for the age of the earth and sun. I don't think we have much in the way of observational evidence in astronomy to conflict with that'. " [10]

The time for frantic recalculation is ***now***! It is time to review all the preconceived ideas that we have been bombarded with since our childhood days about evolution. The Bible tells us "Today if ye will hear his voice, harden not your hearts" (Heb 3:7-8) and "now is the accepted time" (2 Cor 6:2).

There are so many ways of estimating the age of the earth and they all give results in the same order of magnitude as that revealed in creation. They are rejected by evolutionists, because if the earth is *that* young, then evolution could not ever have occurred. Some of these methods are:

- All recorded history and civilisations of the world date back to a maximum of about 6,000 years. Isn't this strange if man, according to evolution, has been around for over 1,000,000 years? [11]
- The oldest living trees in the world dated accurately by annual growth rings are about 4,000 - 5,000 years old, in harmony with the date of the Flood in the Creation model. [12]
- The present world population (about 6 billion people) is in harmony with the date of the Flood. If we start with 8 people who came out of the Ark and apply a growth factor of 2.5 children per family (less than the present rate), we will end up with the present population in about 4,300 years, which takes us back to Noah's time. But if we take the same rate and apply it to only half a million years of evolution of man, there would not be enough surface area on our planet to contain the number of people. [13]
- Dr. Barnes of Texas University, studied the rate of decay of the magnetic field of the earth, using recorded data of scientists over the past 300 years. He found out that if we go back beyond 20,000 years, the heat from the currents causing the magnetic field would have

been so strong as to separate the core from the mantle of the earth. [14]

• Another measure for the age of the earth comes from the moon. When space ships landed on the moon, evolutionists expected the ships to sink in the layer of meteoritic dust that should have accumulated on the surface of the moon over its assumed age of billions of years. They estimated this layer to be at least 16.5 metres deep. But to their disappointment, when Luna landed on the moon, the greatest reading it gave was under 0.5m, showing that the moon is also young. [15]

Figure 6: Depth of Dust on Moon

Further methods estimating the age of the earth [16] to be under 10,000 years in conformity with Genesis are:

Efflux of helium into the atmosphere;
Decay of carbon-14 in pre-Cambrian wood;
Growth of active coral reefs;

Decay of short period comets;
Formation of river deltas;
Influx of nickel, silicon, lead, aluminium, chromium, manganese and other elements to the ocean via rivers.

We must take the book of Genesis seriously. As far as the Bible is concerned no actual dates are given, but all dates must be under 10,000 years, and this is supported by science. True science when examined by those who have not been brainwashed by evolution, agrees with Genesis that the earth is young but tired. "The whole creation groaneth and travaileth in pain" (Rom 8:22).

Figure 7: Age of the Earth

REFERENCES

1. Cook, M. *Prehistory and Earth Models*, Max Parish, London. 1966.
2. Stansfield M. *The Science of Evolution*, MacMillan, New York, 1977. pp. 80-84.
3. Austen, S. "Isotope and Trace Element Analysis of Hypersthene-Normative Basalts from the Quaternary of Uinkaret Plateau, Western Grand Canyon, Arizona", paper presented to the Geological Society of America, 1992.
4. Libby, W.F. *Radiocarbon Dating*, University of Chicago Press, Chicago, 1955, p. 7.
5. Milton, R. *The Facts of Life*, Corgi Books U.K. 1992, pp. 45-49.
6. *Radiocarbon*, Vol. **8** (1966).
7. *Science*, Vol. **224** (1984), pp. 58-61.
8. Robert Lee, "Radiocarbon, Ages in Error", Robert Lee, *Anthropological Journal of Canada*, Vol. **19**, No. **3**, p. 9.
9. Olsson, I.U. "C14 dating and Egyptian chronology", *Proceedings of the Twelfth Nobel Symposium*, John Wiley & Sons Inc., New York, 1970, p. 35.
10. Kazman, R.G. "It's about time: 4.5 billion years", *Geotimes*, Vol. **23**, September 1978, p. 18. Quoting Professor Brew.
11. Morris, H.M. *Scientific Creationism*, Creation Life Publishers, San Diego, California, 1980, pp. 191-193.
12. Morris, H.M. *The Biblical Basis for Modern Science,* Baker Book House, Michigan, 1993, pp. 449-453.
13. ibid. pp. 414-426.
14. Barnes, T.G. *Origin and Destiny of the Earth's Magnetic Field*, Institute for Creation Research, San Diego, 1973, p. 25.
15. Whitcomb, J.C. and DeYoung, D.B. *The Moon. Its Creation, Form and Significance,* Baker Book House, Grand Rapids, Michigan, 1978, pp. 94-95.
16. Morris, H.M. and Parker, G.E. *What is Creation Science?* Master Books, El Cajon, USA 1987, p. 288-291.

Chapter 10

CREATED IN HIS IMAGE - THE MISSING LINK WILL ALWAYS BE MISSING

"And God said, Let us make man in our image, after our likeness" (Gen 1:26).

The Bible tells us that God created Adam in His own image - a special creation. When man sinned, God's love and mercy were such that He provided a way for salvation. We are special in His sight, and He sent His only begotten Son, the Lord Jesus Christ, to die at the cross in our place.

Evolutionists do not accept any of this. According to evolution, human beings are a result of an endless series of accidents, mutations, death, suffering and survival of the fittest. There is no room for the God of love and purpose in their considerations.

For the theory of Evolution to be accepted, there must be billions of fossils of transitional forms. We have seen that not a single transitional form has been found in the fossil record. This is also the case in the supposed evolution of man from ape. Most textbooks, journals, magazines, and science programmes on radio and television claim that the missing link, the ape-man, has been found. Yet when the evidence is examined, not a single one is found to be genuine. Once again the series of premeditated deceptions confirms the great interest Satan takes in spreading the theory of Evolution.

Around the beginning of this century, there was a race among scientists and palaeontologists, whether qualified or amateurs, to find the missing link. They thought that if they could only discover the ape-man, then their names would go down in history as those who gave God the last appearance on the scene of creation. In the back of their minds they wanted to take the place of God. But I regret to say that many of them were willing to use all possible means and ways to achieve this "discovery". They were willing to use frauds and hoaxes, to use any kind of scientific deception - to break all moral codes - to cheat, lie, deceive and even forge in order to attain their aims. But I can state, with complete assurance, that no one has found the ape-man, the missing link for one simple reason - *it does not exist*.

Consider **Java Man** for example, built by Dubois on the evidence of a leg bone, skull cap and three teeth. He concealed for 30 years the fact that he had found "modern" human skulls near it and at the same level. Before his death and after having convinced most of the early sceptics, Dubois confessed that the skull was that of an ape. The deception was revealed only at his deathbed when his conscience was suffering greatly and after he had convinced most evolutionists that he had found the missing link.

Nebraska Man was built on the evidence of a tooth - just think of a scientific theory of the origin of man based on one tooth. Using this tooth, evolutionists developed an idea about Nebraska man, his wife and the tools they used - all from one tooth and a great stretch of imagination! It could have passed as a joke had the picture not been placed in science textbooks and taught as fact and science! Years later it was discovered that the tooth belonged neither to man nor to ape but to a pig! Yet Nebraska man is still taught in many textbooks today as the missing link.

Piltdown Man, discovered in England by Charles Dawson in 1912, was based on a piece of jaw, two molar teeth and a piece of skull. Dawson claimed to have found ape-man and dated the find as half a million years old. In 1953 the hoax was exposed [1], the jaw belonged to a modern day ape, the teeth had been filed down and the bones artificially coloured to deceive the public. The ease with which this fraud, placed in the British Museum for 40 years, fooled the world's greatest authorities illustrates the powerful influence of preconceived ideas among evolutionists.

Peking Man of China, claimed to be ape-man, was built up on evidence of fragments of skull, jaws and teeth. The evidence has since been unaccountably lost! Yet Peking Man is still claimed today as the missing link!

The discoveries of Louis Leaky and Dart of the **Australopithecus** and **Zinjanthropus** were later proved by Richard Leaky and others to be male and female of one type of well known African ape and not ape-man. **Neanderthal Man** and **Cro-Magnon Man** have cranial capacities even bigger than modern man. Scientists today agree that both specimens are true Homo Sapiens (modern man), otherwise they will reverse the theory of Evolution!

It is worth noting at this point that although scientists are aware of the deceptions mentioned above, the alleged ape-men are still found in textbooks and taught to students as science and fact!

Many human skulls have been discovered at levels below the uppermost. If the geologic column is to be taken seriously then skulls of modern man should appear only in the uppermost levels, with any so called ancestors in the levels below. Yet the discoveries of many human skulls below the uppermost levels make modern man contemporary with his alleged ancestors and in some cases even older! A great number of human skulls have been found by specialists who witnessed to the fact that the layers were not disturbed. Yet evolutionists ignore such findings like many others which contradict the feeble theory.

The famous "Lucy", discovered by Johanson in Ethiopia in the 1970s, was claimed to be the missing link (ape-woman!). The claim has since been rejected by famous scientists like Dr Charles Oxnard (Professor of Anatomy and Human Biology) who spent years studying every detail in the most advanced laboratories in the world [2].

The *Weekend Australian* 7-8 May, 1983, described the response of Richard Leaky, the Director of Natural History Museums of Kenya, to the Lucy find:

"Echoing the criticism made of his father's habilis skulls, he added that Lucy's skull was so incomplete that most of it was 'imagination made of plaster of Paris', thus making it impossible to draw any firm conclusion about what species she belonged to" [3].

The famous research anatomist, Prof. Lord Solly Zuckerman, like many other authorities in this field, has questioned the scientific validity of fossil finds. In his book *Beyond the Ivory Tower* he writes:

"The record is so astonishing that it is legitimate to ask whether much science is yet to be found in this field at all" [4].

Alleged Ape Man	Theory built on....	Conclusions
Java Man	3 teeth, Leg Bone, Skull cap	Before the death of Dubois, he confessed it was the skull of an ape and finally admitted this theory was a deception.
Nebraska Man	A single tooth!!	Years later it was discoverd it was neither the tooth of a man or ape, but that of a PIG!
Piltdown Man	2 teeth, Pieces of jaw	After 40 years in The British Museum, in 1950 it was exposed as a hoax.
Peking Man	Evidence similar to Piltdown man	Evidence simply disappeared!
Neanderthal Man		The cranial capacity was greater than modern man, therefore it was "accepted" as Modern Man!
Lucy *"Ape Woman"*	A few bones	Rejected by experts as... ..."*imagination made of plaster of Paris!*"

Figure 8: Missing Link?

The earlier discovery by Richard Leaky in 1973, of modern man aged 2.8 million years old (according to evolutionist dating methods), wiped out all the previous ape-man related findings. Speaking on the find, Leaky said:

"What we have discovered simply wipes out everything we have been taught about human evolution and I have nothing to offer in its place" [5].

What a miserable situation! Keeping in mind the discrepancies and weaknesses of the dating methods, this shows firstly the frail structure of the theory of Evolution, and secondly, that all their ape-men are really a product of their own evolutionary fantasies. Those who promote evolution do so, not because they are so interested in science, but because they want it as an excuse to get rid of God from their lives. They do not want to be answerable to God their Creator. They prefer to be in the image of the ape, who cannot hold them responsible for their deeds and whom they have locked up in cages just in case!

The word of God warns those who take such a dangerous path, and the Holy Spirit pleads with their eternal souls:

"Because that which may be known of God is manifest in them; for God hath shewed it unto them. For the invisible things of him from the creation of the world are clearly seen, being understood by the things that are made, even his eternal power and Godhead; *so that they are without excuse:* Because that, when they knew God, they glorified him not as God, neither were thankful; but became vain in their imaginations, and their foolish heart was darkened. Professing themselves to be wise, they became fools, and changed the glory of the uncorruptible God into an image made like to corruptible man, and ... changed the truth of God into a lie, and worshipped and served the creature more than the Creator, who is blessed for ever. Amen" (Rom 1:19-26).

REFERENCES

1. Vere, F. *Lessons of Piltdown*, EPM, UK 1959.
2. Oxnard, E. *New Perspective on Human Evolution*, University of Washington Press, Seattle and London, 1987, p. 227.
3. *Weekend Australian*, 7-8 May 1983, Magazine, p. 3. quoting R Leaky.
4. Zuckerman, Lord Solly, *Beyond the Ivory Tower*, Taplinger Pub. Co. New York, 1970, p. 64.
5. Gish, D.T. *Evolution: The fossils say NO!*, Creation Life Publishers, San Diego, 1979, p. 149.

Chapter 11
SCIENTISTS WITH A CONSCIENCE

"Ye shall seek me, and find me, when ye shall search for me with all your heart" (Jer 29:13).

Having seen and heard the evidence against evolution, people wonder why scientists still accept it and even promote it.

The answer has been clearly stated by many: "The alternative (special creation) is unthinkable"! A large number of scientists have been brought up on a firm belief in evolution as science and fact. They spend many years of their career trying to research aspects of evolution, and so find it very difficult to stand up and say they have wasted their life proving something which is contradictory to science.

Yet the picture is not so gloomy. Some scientists have been able to write books in their field showing the errors of evolution, and we have quoted a number of them in this book. Some are searching for an alternative with an open mind. Such sincere searchers will no doubt one day find the answer in Creation as the Holy Spirit points them to the wonderful Saviour and Creator, the Lord Jesus Christ. Indeed if one reads the testimony of a number of scientists who were evolutionists, but have seen the light, one cannot but praise God. There are hundreds of scientists in the various fields of science today who are convinced that evolution is a religion and has nothing to do with science. The majority of these are creationists, who find that the Biblical record is a very accurate record of what must have happened in the past, if for no other reason than the fact that the existing natural phenomena fit perfectly within a creation model based on the Biblical account.

Several books have been written by Bible believing scientists who accept the Biblical teachings in their literal sense and show from science that creation is superior to evolution. The titles and authors of such books are detailed in the reference section of this book. There are some who were already christian believers and with their high scientific qualifications they have accepted the authority of the Bible as the perfect word of God from Genesis to Revelation. Amongst them are Dr Henry Morris, who chaired the Civil Engineering Department at Virginia Polytechnic Institute for a number of years. He founded the Institute for Creation Research in 1970, dedicated to promoting scientific and Biblical creationism through a program of research, writing, and teaching. He wrote a number of books on this subject including the famous book *The Genesis Flood* [1], co-authored with J. Whitcomb, which started the scientific creationism debate and provided many answers to those who are searching for the truth. Another author is Dr Duane Gish, who has a PhD in Biochemistry from the University of California, Berkeley, USA. He spent years in biochemical and biomedical research at top American colleges and medical centres, and is the author and co-author of numerous technical articles in his field. He resigned to become Associate Director of the Institute for Creation Research. He has lectured on "Creation or Evolution" all around the world and has written a number of books on this subject, most famous amongst them *Evolution: The Fossils Say NO!* [2]. I thank the Lord for both these great men of God and men of science. I was greatly helped by their writings, research and uncompromising acceptance of the Bible as the perfect word of God.

Others were evolutionists before coming to a personal knowledge of the Creator and Saviour through various means including reading the works of the two authors mentioned above. I have heard Dr Gary Parker give his testimony. He was a biology teacher and had written a number of textbooks used in many schools in the United States of America. He was convinced that evolution is science until he started questioning it. After reading a number of books on the scientific evidence for creation and against evolution, he saw the light. He now writes books on creation and lectures all round the world on the authority of the Bible, and against the religious theory of Evolution.

A number of writers who are not creationists, and in some cases do not (yet) believe in God, have recently written books that show from their field of specialisation that evolution is a non-starter as far as science is concerned! Some of those writers propose alternative theories, while others leave the stage without answers. Our prayer is that they will find the answer to their questions in the Bible, like many others before them.

It is worth mentioning some of these writers and books:

1. **Dr Michael Denton** author of *Evolution: A Theory In Crisis*, published in 1986.

   On the cover flap it says: "This authoritative and remarkably accessible book by a molecular biologist shows how rapidly accumulating evidence is threatening the basic assumptions of orthodox Darwinism".

   The question posed in this book by Denton, who has two earned doctorates, sums it up: "Is it really credible that random processes could have constructed a reality, the smallest element of which - a functional protein or gene - is complex beyond our own creative capacities, a reality which is the very antithesis of chance, which excels in every sense anything produced by the intelligence of man?" [3].

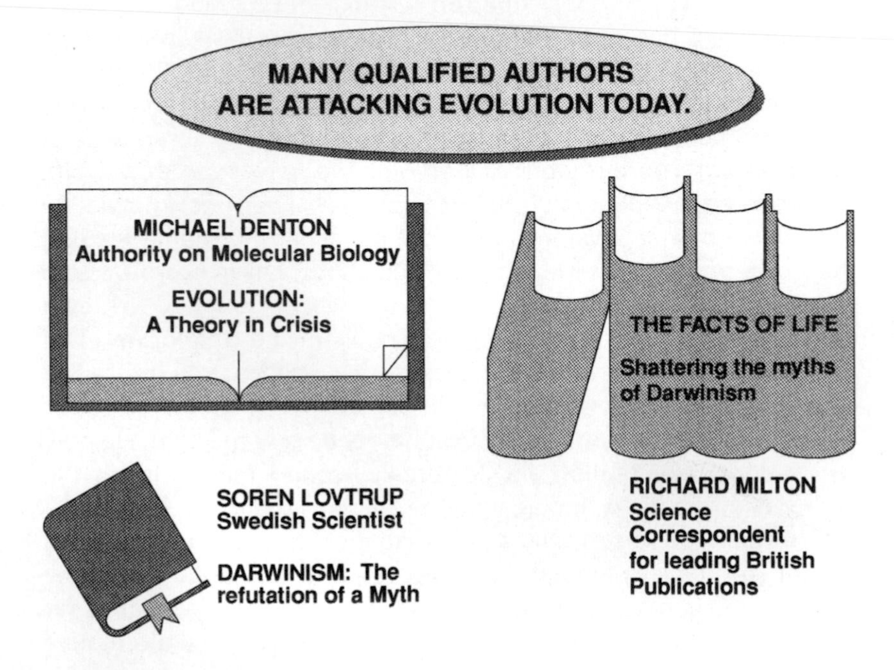

Figure 9: Books Criticising Evolution

2. **Richard Milton** author of *The Facts of Life: Shattering the Myths of Darwinism*, published in 1992.

Milton combines a background as an engineer with experience as a newspaper editor reporting on scientific developments.

Milton says in his book: "I do not belong to any church or religious group". But he stresses that the reason he did so much research on this subject was because he had a daughter, then 9 years old. "I am seriously concerned, on purely rational grounds, that generations of school and university teachers have been led to accept speculation as scientific theory and faulty data as scientific fact" [4].

Milton writes on the world of scientific investigation: "a world that I regularly write about in my job as science reporter and where many discoveries have been made in the last two decades that have an important bearing on evolution theory, but have received little publicity" [5].

Milton concludes his book with the following statement: "As scientists begin to drift away from neo-Darwinist ideas in growing numbers, the revision of Darwinism at the public level is long overdue, and is a process that I believe has already started" [6].

3. **Soren Lovtrup** author of *Darwinism: the Refutation of a Myth*, published in 1987.

This Swedish scientist wrote in his book: "I believe one day the Darwinian myth will be ranked the greatest deceit in the history of science" [7].

REFERENCES

1. Whitcomb, J.C. and Morris, H.M. *The Genesis Flood*, Presbyterian and Reformed Publishing, 1961.
2. Gish, D.T. *Evolution: The Fossils Say NO!*, Creation Life Publishers, San Diego, 1979.
3. Denton, M. *Evolution: A Theory in Crisis*, Adler and Adler, Bethesda, Maryland, 1985.
4. Milton, R. *The Facts of Life: Shattering the Myths of Darwinism*, Corgi Books, U.K. 1992.

5. ibid. p. 16.
6. ibid. p. 299.
7. Gish, D.T. *Challenge of the Fossil Record*, Creation Science Movement, U.K. Pamphlet 293, 1993. Quoting Soren Lovtrup.

Chapter 12

NO COMPROMISE!

Before the theory of Evolution had the popular support of many so-called scientists, every christian believer accepted the Genesis record in the Bible literally, without questioning that the earth was young, or the literal 6-day account of creation as it appears in the Bible. Then Satan used his oldest trick; get believers to doubt the Bible and their faith will be shattered. He convinced Eve in the Garden: it worked; why shouldn't it work again? This time Satan developed a new strategy; after all he has been to all the universities in the world and knows how powerful science is. He used evolution to get people, including many Christians, to doubt the word of God. He was able to fabricate evidence "... for he is a liar and the father of it" (John 8:44). Sadly he succeeded to a great extent. Unbelievers had the support of "science" to justify their life of sin and rebellion against the Creator, while believers struggled to compromise between the Bible and what some thought to be the claims of science.

Panic theories were thought up in haste: the Day-Age theory, the Gap theory, Theistic Evolution and others. The aim of all such theories was to fit the billions of evolutionary years into the Bible. Although I have no doubt that many of those who developed such theories did so with good intentions, yet each one of those compromise theories contradicts both the word of God and science.

We are going to discuss the problems with such theories. I do not seek to undermine any particular teaching. My aim is simply to pass on to you what the Lord has shown me from the Bible and after years of study of this subject.

1. The Day-Age Theory

The aim of this theory was to incorporate the geologic ages of evolution within the six days of creation, by saying each day is a million or even a billion years. In fact it cannot incorporate evolution - because the days of creation are not in the same order as the geologic fossil record. There are over twenty discrepancies between them! For example:

- Plant life appears first in Genesis, but comes later on according to evolution.
- Fish and birds were created in the same day in Genesis. According to evolution, fish gave rise to reptiles which developed into mammals and birds over millions of years.
- The sun, moon, and stars were made on the fourth day. Evolution requires them to be there before anything in order to start the life process.
- Plant life was created on the third day, followed by the sun on the fourth day. If the time between those two days was a billion years as the theory claims, then plants must have stayed a billion years without the sunlight.
- Similarly, insects necessary for pollination were created on the sixth day! Was that three days later or three billion years later?
- God told man to give names to all land animals and to exercise dominion over every organism He had created (Gen 1:28). According to the geologic age system, many such organisms were already extinct for ages before man appeared!
- According to the Bible there was no rain at least until the time of man's appearance if not until the flood (Gen 2:5; Heb 11:7). Geologists say that rains have existed since the earth first cooled.
- The summary in Gen 2:1-3 says that all the "host" of the things God "created and made" was finished in six days, and God stopped any further work. According to Genesis, creation work has stopped since the end of day number six. This is in complete contrast to the claim of modern biologists and geologists, that the same processes used to bring the world into being are still in operation today.

Looking at the Day-Age theory from a biblical point of view, it requires misinterpretation of the word of God.

The original word *yom* in Hebrew, Aramaic, and Arabic, refers to a 24-hour period. It was stressed over and over again, that it was the evening and morning; an actual day! (Gen 1:5, 8, 13, 19, 23, 31).

The word day (*yom*) in fact was defined by God Himself the very first time it was used, in Genesis 1:5: "God called the light day". Hence in the context, the day means the succession of day and night, or light and darkness.

Our pattern of life of six days work and one day rest is taken from God's six days of creation and one day of rest. No Christian could have ever dreamt of such a theory had it not been for fear that evolution might be right!

2. The Gap Theory

In light of the weaknesses found within the Day-Age theory, some people invented another theory called the Gap theory. The Gap theory proposes that God originally created the heavens and the earth as recorded in Genesis 1:1, then there was a judgement, after which God started His new six-day creation. Between Genesis 1:1 and 1:2 gap theorists can place all the fossil record which will correspond to the geologic column spanning millions of years, thus providing adequate room for evolution!

Let us be in no doubt that this was another panic solution to the growing threat of evolution in the early days of the publication of *The Origin of the Species* [1]. The man who was probably most responsible for the origin and popularity of the Gap theory was Thomas Chalmers (1780-1847), who was a preacher and theologian in the Church of Scotland. His basic ideas were taken up and developed by famous people like Darby, Scofield, Newberry, Larkin and others.

The idea was very tempting to develop, and each contributor developed some aspect of it, finding abundant room for tackling the issues of Satan, angels, pre-Adamic earth, pre-Noah flood, and many more issues that were "solved" as a bonus on top of the compromise with what was then believed to be a scientific challenge to the authority of the Bible.

Almost all the Gap theory promoters or supporters state clearly the reason behind their thinking. Scofield, for example, brings out the motivation for promoting the theory: "that no conflict of science with the Genesis cosmogony remains" [2]. Larkin in his book *The Greatest Book on Dispensational Truth in the World* writes:

"Science demands thousands of years for the formation of the earth and all the time it demands is given to it in the sublime words of Genesis 1:1" [3].

The attempts to compromise with evolution in such a theory led to an endless number of assumptions: God creating a physical creation of bone structure and flesh for the habitation of angels! Or God creating a perfect earth in the endless past for the habitation of a race of men without any souls! It also led to the misinterpretation of the original text to fit in with the gap at any cost and to the denial of the fact that the flood in the days of Noah was universal!

Unknowingly, the Gap theory has resulted in the glorification of the power of Satan! It has painted a picture of God which contradicts what the Bible tells us about His justice by assuming that He punished the world for the sin of Satan and the fallen angels. It has ignored a basic verse in the Bible that by Adam sin came into the world and by sin death (Rom 5:12), *and* that Adam was the *first* man (1 Cor 15:45)!

How can we accept a compromise theory, based on assumptions, myths, creative imagination, contradicting the straight forward interpretation of the word of God, put forward by mortal men, and reject the words of the Creator Himself, assuming that He couldn't have meant what He said! We are rightly indignant when so-called christian institutions tamper with translations in order to support an idea (for example John 1:1), and yet a forced translation of foundational passages is casually accepted to fit the gap!

We shall look briefly at some basic issues that expose the weaknesses of the Gap theory:

- One of the major reasons for the Gap theory thinking was the idea that the fossil record consists of extinct animals which must have belonged to a totally alien world. However, we know today that although the fossil shows some extinct animals and plants, the majority of fossils discovered have not changed from the living species of today. Many fossils have embarrassed the evolutionists who assumed they were extinct by suddenly appearing alive and well, so they gave them the name "living fossils"!
- Dinosaurs are another example of this. They created a problem for the Gap theory promoters because they did not understand them

and believed the claims of evolutionists at the time that dinosaurs became extinct 70 million years ago!! Their size made them convincingly (for the Gapists), part of a previous creation. Today we know that dinosaurs are kinds of lizards and we know much about the conditions of life before the flood to understand that there is nothing supernatural about them that requires a pre-Adamic creation to explain. We also know that Job saw a dinosaur which was called by its real name *behemoth*! (Job 40:15). See Section III for more details.

- There are human remains in the geologic column and footprints alongside dinosaurs and trilobites, showing that human beings like us lived alongside the other extinct animals, large and small. Evolutionists have kept quiet about this!
- According to the Gap theorists, pre-Adamic men perished due to the sin of Satan, which took place in heaven anyway. What kind of a picture does this paint of our God?
  The theological implication of the gap is that sin is not the cause of death. The finger is then pointed at God for bringing in a system of decay and death in His creation as a process to bring about man's existence. The Bible teaches us that death came in as a result of man's sin.
- If we accept fossils before Adam, we deny the basic teaching of the Bible:
  (a) "The first man Adam was made a living soul" (1 Cor 15:45);
  (b) "Wherefore, as by one man sin entered into the world and death by sin; and so death passed upon all men" (Rom 5:12).
- The Bible tells us that God created Adam out of the "dust of the earth" and observed him as "very good". According to the Gap theory, God must have created Adam from an earth full of fossils, bones and destruction. Yet when He finished His creation work, "God saw everything that he had made and behold it was very good" (Gen 1:31). Either the theory is wrong, or it *makes God a liar*! (1 John 5:10).
- The flood in the days of Noah is the staunchest argument against evolution; it is this historical fact that evolutionists vigorously want to deny. By taking up the Gap theory as proposed by *men*, the

believer gives much ground to the enemy, with a false sense of satisfaction regarding the scriptural rigidity of his argument. The account of the flood is given in so much detail in the Bible both to emphasise its importance and the fact that it was **universal:** "And the waters prevailed exceedingly, upon the earth; and ***all*** the high hills, that were under the ***whole*** heaven, were covered. Fifteen cubits upward did the waters prevail; and the mountains were covered" (Gen 7:19-20). The exact depth as well as the exact dimensions of the ark are recorded for our teaching (Rom 15:4). The Lord Jesus spoke about Noah's universal flood as a fact, comparing the flood with future destruction: "And knew not until the flood came, and took them ***all*** away" (Matt 24:39).

- Once again, this theory requires changing some words in the original text. For example in Genesis 1:2 :
  (a) The words *"was void"* are changed to *"became void"*, which is not justified when the original is considered.
  (b) Also the word *"without form"* is changed to *"ruined"* with no justification.

Let us keep in mind that the Gap theory is an idea about scripture, and not truth in itself. There is no shame or weakness in reassessing the validity of such ideas in the light of what the word of God actually says. The Scriptures, and what generations before have written are not the same thing!

The Gap theory has arisen from an era of compromise, when Christians were on the run from the vicious attack of humanism on the church. Many public debates between Christians and humanists were won by people such as Huxley, bringing embarrassment to Christians. The need to hold on to truth brought about compromises - a fact admitted freely by major supporters. However, those who believe in the Gap theory unknowingly contradict the word of God.

The Gap theory brought up more questions than it answered and went against basic tenets of Scripture. Christians had to hold on to inconsistencies which weakened the faith of some and led many, especially university students, away from the faith of their fathers. It also meant that Christians who accepted the Gap had to be silent as to the truth of the flood, having placed all the fossils long before the days of Noah. Evolutionists as we have seen are keen to deny Noah's flood. We come back to Peter's second epistle, "for this they *wilfully forget*". We must wilfully remind them!

But finally, God Himself refuses to be misunderstood on this matter! In Exodus 20:11, in a section of literal, legal text, the Lord Himself states : "... for in six days the LORD made *heaven and earth, the sea, and all that in them is*, and rested the seventh day".

In Exodus 31:17 the Lord gives the final words of the law: "... for in six days the LORD made heaven and earth, and on the seventh day he rested, and was refreshed".

To leave us in no doubt as to the authorship of such a revelation, the Holy Spirit records in the following verse: "He gave Moses two tablets of the testimony, tablets of stone, written with the finger of God".

God created the earth, a void mass without form and in darkness, on the eve of the first day. "Let there be light ..." and the first morning started. What a morning, what a Creator! One cannot help but bend the knee at His throne and say: "Thou art worthy, O Lord, to receive glory and honour and power: for thou hast created all things..." (Rev 4:11).

The simple conclusion is that this theory, much popularised amongst Christians by Scofield and others, as a way of accommodating evolution in Genesis, contradicts the literal translation and the spirit of the Bible. It is very clear that the Gap theory must be rejected by all Christians.

3.Theistic Evolution

Evolutionists had a problem in explaining the first cell, so Christians said : let us say the first cell was created by God and then He left it all to evolution!!

Immediately, one can see the problems. On the one hand, evolutionists do not accept the compromise, because their objective is to get rid of God completely!

On the other hand, as Christians, how can we accept such a helpless, incapable God? Just imagine for a moment; God creates the first cell and then sits back and waits millions of years for the mutations to happen! Then the trilobite appears! Another 200 million years, the frog! Great! And so on until man "evolves" after millions of years of struggle, suffering, death and survival of the fittest.

This is not our God! This is not the God the Bible tells us about.

The Bible speaks of an Almighty Creator and Designer, a God of power who "made the earth by his power"; a God of wisdom who "established the world by his wisdom"; and a God of discretion who "stretched out the heavens by his discretion" (Jer 10:12); a God who designed and created all things to crown them by man, created specially in His own image.

Now this is our God! And we do not accept to believe any compromise theories that reduce the greatness of our Almighty Creator.

All or Nothing

"But continue thou in the things which thou hast learned and hast been assured of, knowing of whom thou hast learned them: And that from a child thou hast known the holy scriptures which are able to make thee wise" (2 Tim 3:14-15).

As believers we cannot question the finger of God. We hold with six literal days. The earth was created on the first day. If we insist on compromises, we are contradicting the finger of God. My heart has been challenged with the majesty of God's word, and I'm sure your heart will respond: "All scripture is given by inspiration of God" (2 Tim 3:16).

True science agrees with the Bible and contradicts evolution. The millions and billions of years are not supported by science. True science agrees with a young earth of several thousand years old and a literal six-day creation. The most scientific statement of origins is still, "In the beginning God created the heaven and the earth" (Gen 1:1).

I have often been criticised for taking a dogmatic view on these issues. My answer is that this is what God says in the Bible and if He meant something else He would have told us that. The Bible is not subject to our human interpretation. With the help of the Holy Spirit, we can expound the Scriptures, but not interpret them according to our fallible and limited minds. As believers who spend years of our lives with the Lord, talking to Him in prayer and He to us through His word the Bible, having seen Him work in our lives, having placed our entire faith on His death at the cross of Calvary in our place, based on what we read in the Bible, if after all those years we still cannot accept that His word is *perfect*, then there is something wrong in this relationship which needs our urgent attention. What better place to sort it out than at Golgotha, where our *Creator* became our personal *Saviour* at a cost beyond the grasp of our human minds.

So what does all this mean to us? Those who are Christians - who have already accepted Christ as Lord and Saviour, lift up your heads! For our Creator is great! Trust in the word of God. "Heaven and earth shall pass away: but my words shall not pass away" (Luke 21:33).

The Bible is a *wonderful* book. It is a *spiritual* book, but whatever subject it touches upon whether astronomy, physics, mathematics, medicine, or history... it is an *authority* on that subject. Take it all.

It is *perfect.* We do not need compromises. The Lord Jesus taught us not to compromise with evil, and evolution *is* evil! Take the word of God as it is - God created the heavens and the earth in six *literal* days, several thousand years ago. He crowned it all by the creation of man in His own image: a special creation *not the result of an accident.* Unless we, as Christians, come to accept this basic truth, without fear and without compromise, we will never experience the full blessings of our Creator and Saviour, Jesus Christ.

REFERENCES

1. Darwin, C. *The Illustrated Origin of the Species*, (Abridged and introduced by Richard Leaky), Book Club Associates, London, 1979.
2. Scofield, C.I. *The Scofield Reference Bible*, Oxford University Press, London, 1917, notes on pp. 3-4.
3. Larkin, C. *The Greatest Book on Dispensational Truth in the World,* Clarence Larkin Estate, Glenside, USA, 1918. p. 22.

Chapter 13
EVIDENCE THAT DEMANDS A CREATOR!

To sum it all up: evolution contradicts science. It is a religion - but an inferior religion and an inferior science. What the world really shows is evidence of a Creator who created us in His image!

Look at the world around. Look at the sun, the stars and the heavens - and praise God the Creator. It is no accident this vast universe - it is no accident that our earth is the only place fit for life. It is no accident that the distance between our earth and the sun makes it the only planet where life can exist and prosper.

It is no accident that the earth's axis of rotation is tilted 23.5° to cause the four seasons, or that the earth rotates once every 24 hours producing day and night without getting tired. It is no accident that our atmosphere has the exact thickness and composition to serve as a filter to ultraviolet rays and cosmic rays that are harmful to life.

Consider the brain! The human brain is known to be superior to the most sophisticated modern computers of the world. It is known today that the human brain is composed of about 12 billion neurones. Each neurone is connected to about 10 thousand other neurones giving a total of 120 trillion connections in the human brain - the most sophisticated and complicated arrangement known to man.

Or what about the eye? When Darwin considered the human eye, he had to write: "To suppose that the eye could have been formed by natural selection, seems, I freely confess, absurd in the highest degree". This is the testimony of the father of evolution.

In the world around us everything calls for a Designer - a great omnipotent Designer who can co-ordinate everything; everything calls for a Creator. "The heavens declare the glory of God; and the firmament sheweth his handywork" (Ps 19:1).

For any readers who haven't yet made up their minds concerning this issue, I hope I have been able to direct your thoughts and minds to a reconsideration of Biblical creation - and if you are willing to look into it seriously, then I have good news for you.

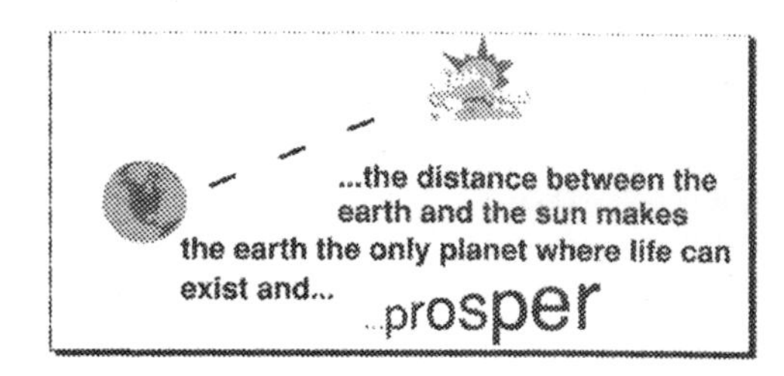

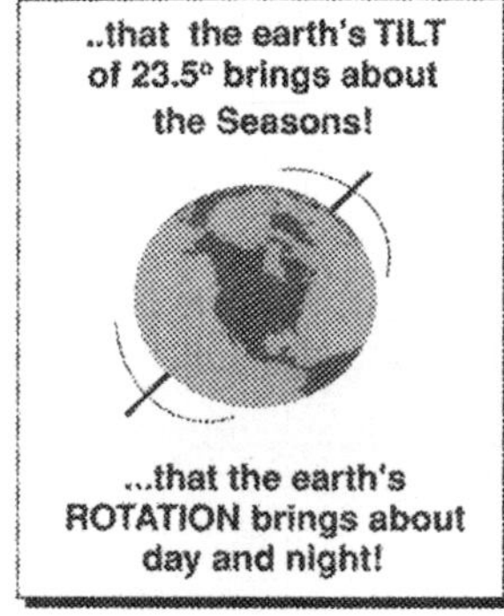

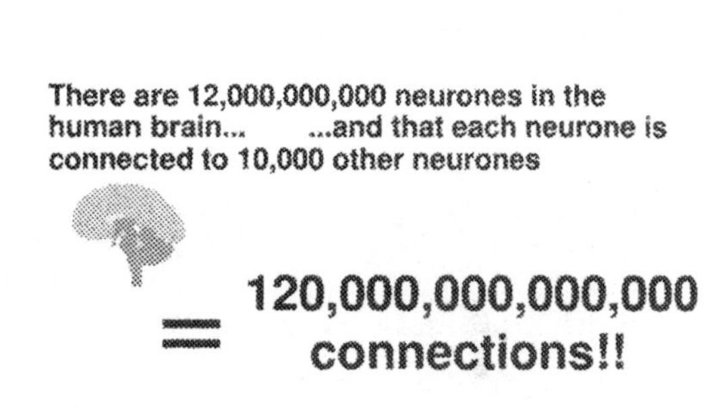

Figure 10: Some Remarkable Facts

This Creator of the universe, the Lord Jesus Christ, through whom and by whom all things were created - this Creator who holds the whole universe in one hand, holds you in the other. This Creator cares for you as much as He cares for all His creation, because He created you in His own image to live with Him forever.

We saw how accurate is the word of God. The Bible tells us that Adam and Eve disobeyed God in the Garden of Eden. It also tells us that since that time sin has entered the world and that "all have sinned, and come short of the glory of God" (Rom 3:23) - this "all" includes you and me.

God also says "the wages of sin is death" (Rom 6:23). There is no way we can come back to the holy God while we are in our sins - we cannot approach Him by our own good works, for they are "as filthy rags" (Isa 64:6).

Because God's love is so great, He had prepared a way for our salvation. He sent His Son, the Lord Jesus Christ, to this world of ours.

He lived a perfect sinless life and was therefore the only one who could bring us back to the holy God.

To show us His love, He accepted to exchange His crown of glory for a crown of thorns that made His holy head bleed. He accepted to exchange the singing of angels in heaven, "Holy... Holy... Holy...", for the cries of the angry crowds in Jerusalem saying, "Crucify Him, crucify Him".

He accepted to carry His cross to the place of the skull, the hill of death, and to allow men to nail Him to it - men whom His own hands had made out of the dust - because He loved us!

There hung up between heaven and earth He paid the price for your sins and my sins - as God laid all our sins on His Son during those hours of darkness culminating in the cry from the cross: "It is finished". The way for our salvation was opened for whosoever will. God showed that He accepted the sacrifice of His Son, in that He raised the Lord Jesus from the dead on the third day, triumphant over sin and Satan and death. "O death where is thy sting? O grave, where is thy victory?" (1 Cor 15:55).

This Creator can be your own personal Saviour if you believe in His work at the cross in your place and ask Him to forgive you your sins and live in your heart.

I invite you to make your choice now. If you choose creation - if you accept the Creator as you own personal Saviour - then you have found the truth you are searching for, because Jesus said, "I am the truth" (John 14:6). Finding the truth is finding freedom, for He said, "Ye shall know the truth, and the truth shall make you free" (John 8:32). This is the true freedom - freedom from the power of sin and Satan - freedom from fear of that unknown called death.

What better words to sum it all up than those of the Creator Himself from the Bible:

"In the beginning God created the heaven and the earth" (Gen 1:1); and "God so loved the world, that he gave his only begotten Son, that whosoever believeth in him should not perish, but have everlasting life" (John 3:16).

PART III - EVIDENCE FOR THE FLOOD AND NOAH'S ARK

Chapter 14

THE WORLD THAT THEN WAS!

"And God saw every thing that he had made, and, behold, it was very good" (Gen 1:31).

As we read the book of Genesis, we are amazed by the record of life before the days of Noah. People lived much longer than they do today, had many children and appeared to be much healthier. We read for example about Methuselah, who lived 969 years (Gen 5:27). We are told also that there were giants in the earth in those days (Gen 6:4).

To understand this, let us consider the Biblical account of how the world was before the flood.

Majestically the Bible tells us "In the beginning God created the heaven and the earth" (Gen 1:1) and it goes on to tell us what God created on each day.

Let us concentrate on day number two. On that day God said: "Let there be a firmament in the midst of the waters, and let it divide the waters from the waters. And God made the firmament, and divided the waters which were under the firmament from the waters which were above the firmament: and it was so..." (Gen 1:6,7).

It is interesting to note that the original word for 'firmament' gives the meaning of a thin sheet compressed or pounded out and stretched.

This could well represent the earth before the flood, with a firmament consisting of water vapour suspended as a canopy several miles above the earth. This configuration [1] would have done some wonderful things:

1. The fibre-optical transfer of light through such a canopy would have meant that the greater penetration of light would produce varying shades of pink. Research has revealed that it is pink light which optimally triggers the growth of cells within plants.[2] This may explain the presence within the fossil record of such things as giant mosses called lepidodendrons over 30 m (100 ft) tall, while the modern variety grows to a maximum height of 40 cm (16 inches) ! No wonder God ordered the animals, when they were created, to eat only plants which were in abundance.

2. Researchers have been able to approximate the effect of such a canopy on the atmospheric pressure. They estimate that before the flood the atmospheric pressure would have been about twice the level it is today due to the fact that all the gases would have been compressed below the canopy. Also, the percentage of oxygen in the atmosphere was higher. This has been confirmed by the fact that air bubbles trapped in amber in the fossil record before the flood showed 30% oxygen content compared to 20% today. These conditions are the optimum conditions for life.

Hyperbaric medical chambers at greater than atmospheric pressure and with enhanced oxygen content have recently become a useful medical tool. Scientists are finding that people with open wounds, placed in such chambers heal overnight rather than during a couple of weeks. A person pronounced clinically dead from carbon monoxide poisoning recovered within three weeks in a hyperbaric chamber at Texas A & M University medical research centre, with no impairment of memory. A similar incident has been documented in 1996 in the UK. Such treatment restores memory loss, reverses the ravages of senility and helps stroke victims.

Hyperbaric chambers are now being used increasingly in medical research centres around the world, simulating some aspects of the pre-flood perfect world; namely higher atmospheric pressure and enhanced oxygen content.

As for plants, a tomato plant grown for two years in such chambers reached a height of over 5 m (16 ft), bore 930 tomatoes and continued to grow [3]. The fossil record tells us that giantism was common among plants prior to the flood. The Bible talks about giantism before the flood (Gen 6:4) and science confirms the accuracy of the word of God.

Figure 11: A Perfect World

PRE-FLOOD WORLD MODEL

And God saw everything that he had made, and behold it was very good.

Genesis 1:31

- **Twice Atmospheric Pressure**
- **30% Oxygen**
- **Filtration of Harmful Radiation**

3. Another effect of this canopy would have been the filtration of harmful radiation. The American Environmental Protection Agency has announced that in a matter of decades, one out of three persons will die of cancer due to increased ultraviolet radiation. Before the flood all harmful radiation would have been filtered out by the water canopy enhancing health by reducing harmful mutation rates. [4]

No wonder human beings and animals lived longer before the flood, had healthier lives and enjoyed the perfect atmosphere, for God pronounced His creation as "very good". People ridicule the great ages of men in the Bible before the flood. But with the perfect conditions discussed above there is no problem. We have seen the effect of some simulated pre-flood conditions on the healing processes of the human body as well as on what had become a downgraded tomato seed and contaminated soil through ages of deterioration since the flood. Why should we then question the longevity of people and their health conditions before the flood as they enjoyed God's perfect creation?

Sadly this utopia did not last too long. Something happened to change all of this. "God looked upon the earth, and, behold it was corrupt" (Gen 6:12). God saw the evil of men and He decided to put an end to these perfect conditions. All life was to perish except those who would go into the ark with Noah and his family, because Noah was righteous in the sight of God (Gen 7:1).

REFERENCES

1. Baugh, C. *Panorama of Creation*, Creation Publication Services, Texas, 1992, pp. 42-64.
2. ibid. pp. 51-52.
3. ibid. pp. 70-71.
4. Ham, K., Snelling, A. and Wieland, C. *The Answers Book,* Master Books, El Cajon, CA, USA, 1992, p. 122.

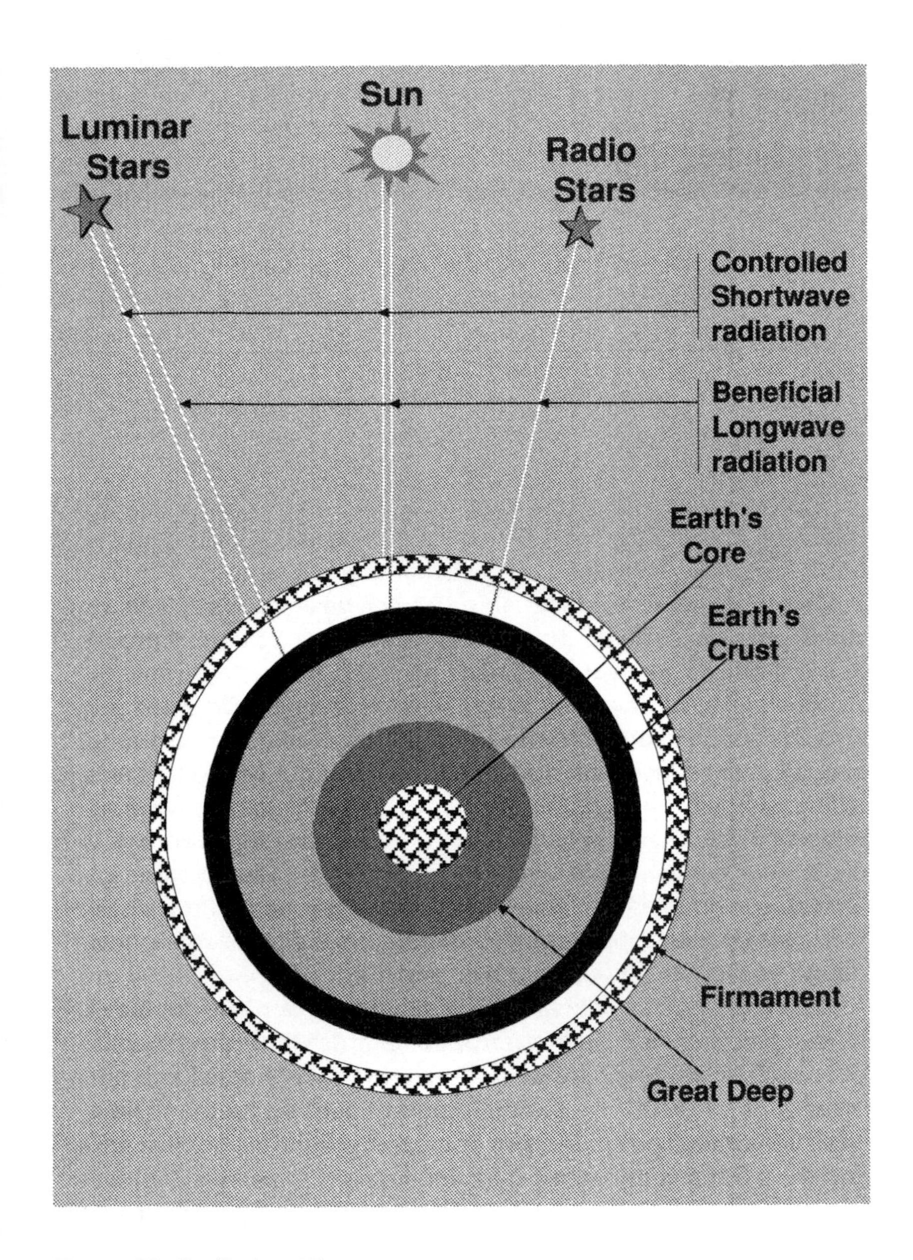

Figure 12: Radiation Filters

Chapter 15
THE AMAZING ARK

When I was a child, I was told the story of the flood from the Bible. It was fascinating trying to imagine Noah and his ark and all those animals. At the same time it was frightening to think of the people who were left outside as God shut the door and the flood began.

As a child I believed the story. But as I grew older, at school and later at university, most students, teachers and professors made fun of the story and accused me of being unscientific about the subject.

This led me on a long journey of research. I wanted the truth. What does true science say? Who is really brainwashed? Could a universal flood really have happened and is the ark fact or fiction?

The years of research in this subject have brought one clear conclusion: the evidence points in favour of the account of the flood as it appears in the book of Genesis.

When I was at university doing a course in hydraulic engineering, we were asked to investigate and find out the best dimensions for a body in water to withstand extreme conditions at sea. We came out with a variety of designs. But to my amazement, the professor (who was not a Christian) said, "I should not tell you this, but the best dimensions can be found in the Bible. They are those of Noah's ark. That ship cannot sink." I was thrilled with that comment and asked the question which no one dared to answer: Who told Noah how to design an unsinkable ship?

God told Noah to build an ark: "Make thee an ark of gopher wood; rooms shalt thou make in the ark, and shalt pitch it within and without with pitch...The length of the ark shall be three hundred cubits, the breadth of it fifty cubits, and the height of it thirty cubits. A window shalt thou make to the ark, and in a cubit shalt thou finish it above; and the door of the ark shalt thou set in the side thereof; with lower, second, and third stories shalt thou make it" (Gen 6:14-16).

The dimensions of the ark have been analysed by experts in the field of hydraulic engineering. Dr Henry Morris, who chaired civil engineering departments in top American universities, after careful analysis of these dimensions came to the conclusion that it is almost impossible to capsize [1].

Stability Analysis of Noah's Ark

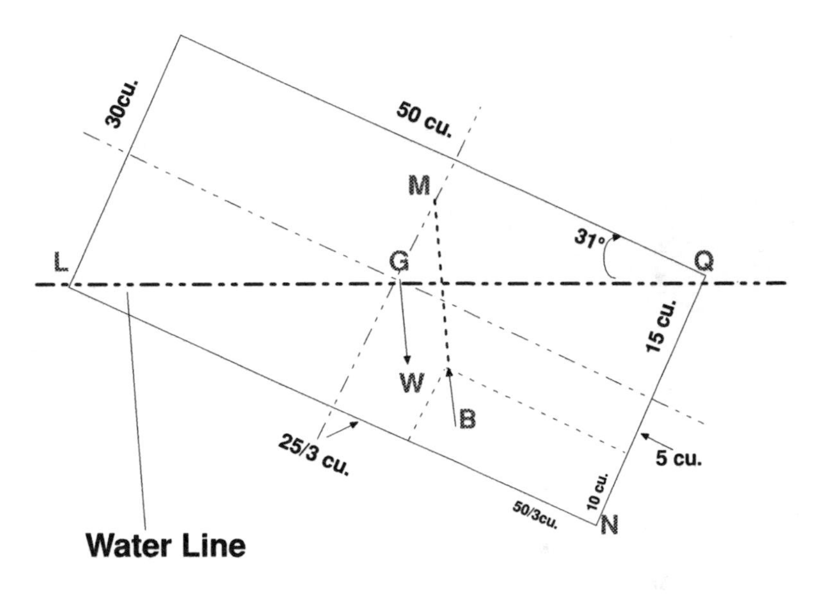

W = weight of ark acting through centre of gravity G

B = buoyant force acting through centre of gravity of water displaced

M = metacentre, where line of action of B intersects central axis, above G

Figure 13: Stability Analysis of Noah's Ark

Analysis of stability has been carried out using a cross section of the ark and the forces and moments acting on it as it is tilted about by violent storms. They show that the buoyant force tending to right it, always acts outside the weight force tending to capsize it. The result is it will always return to its normal floating position. [2]

Furthermore, its ratio of length to width of 6 to 1 (300 cubits to 50 cubits) tend to keep it from being subjected to wave forces of equal magnitude over its whole length, since wave fields tend to occur in broken and varying patterns, rather than in a series of long uniform crest-trough sequences. Any vortex action to which it might occasionally be subjected would also tend to be resisted and broken up by its 6 to 1 length to width ratio.

Therefore the ratios God gave Noah for the ark are the best ratios for stability, pitching and rolling. The ark was not designed for speed. Noah was not in a hurry to go anywhere! In fact he wanted to stay as close as possible to the land he knew.

It is interesting to know that Brunel, the great British inventor, designed his famous ship in 1844 nearly 4000 years after Noah and called it "The Great Britain" [3]. It had almost identical ratios of length: width: height, to Noah's ark: 322 ft x 51 ft x 32.5 ft (98 m x 15.5 m x 10 m). Brunel had the accumulated knowledge of generations of shipbuilders to draw upon. The ark was the first of its kind.

The ark had the capacity to accommodate all the "passengers" that God asked Noah to take on board with ample free space left. Some very simple calculations will confirm this fact: [4]

Dimensions of the ark : 300 cubits x 50 cubits x 30 cubits. Using a small cubit equivalent of 17.5 inches the ark will be:

- 437 ft x 73 ft x 44 ft, or 133 m x 22 m x 13.5 m
- Volume = 1,396,000 cu ft, or 39,500 cu m
- This is equivalent to 522 standard American railroad stock cars of 2670 cu ft capacity, which can carry about 200 sheep in two decks.
- Enough to carry over 125,000 sheep-size animals.

THE ARK WAS

300 Cubits x 50 Cubits x 30 Cubits
A small Cubit was 17.5 inches

- **SIZE ~ 437ft x 73ft x 44ft**
- **VOLUME ~ 1,396,000 cu.ft.**

It was

- $1\frac{1}{2}$ times the size of a football pitch
- taller than a 3-storey building
- large enough to carry 125,000 sheep-size animals

There are about 18,000 species of land animals alive today

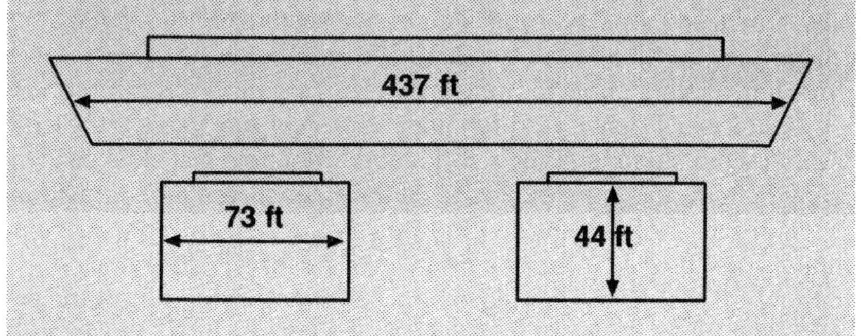

Figure 14: Dimensions of the Ark

There are about 18,000 species of land animals alive today. If we allow for all the extinct species and any others we missed in the count, and take two of each and seven of some as God instructed Noah, the total comes to less than 50,000; leaving plenty room for food, and perhaps all the third floor for Noah and his family to live in and lots of free space to play football and other favourite family games!

The Bible does not tell us how long Noah spent building the ark. However there is no reason to reject the figure of 100 years which is taken as the difference between Noah's age of 500 recorded in Genesis 5:32 and his age of 600 when the flood started as recorded in Genesis 7:11. This is a logical span of time to build a huge ship, considering the limited technology and equipment they had at that time. It also goes well with explaining 1 Peter 3:20 about the long-suffering of God, waiting in the days of Noah while the ark "was a preparing"! The fact that Lamech, Noah's father, died five years before the flood cannot be used to restrict the construction time to an impossible five years even with today's equipment. God's intervention in many aspects of the flood is clear from the account. He designed the ark but left the construction for Noah and his company to complete! The Bible does not record everything that God told Noah and He could have told Noah that his father would not live till the flood.

REFERENCES

1. Morris, H.M. *The Biblical Basis for Modern Science,* Baker Book House, Michigan, 1993, p. 295.
2. ibid. pp. 293-295.
3. Whitcomb, J.C. *The World that Perished*, Baker Book House, Michigan, 1993, p. 22.
4. Morris (Ref. 1) pp. 291-292.

Chapter 16
THE FLOOD

God spoke and three things happened:

1. "All the fountains of the great deep were broken up" (Gen 7:11).
2. "The windows of heaven were opened" (Gen 7:11).
3. "And the rain was upon the earth forty days and forty nights" (Gen 7:12).

Let us first consider two common questions:

- Where did the water come from ?
- Where did the water that covered the mountains go?

The answer to the first question, "where did the water come from?", is simple: it was the water held up in the water canopy from day number two of the creation week. God had it there for protecting His creation and providing the perfect atmosphere for man's prosperity and health. But when, as far as God was concerned, man's disobedience reached its limits, that same canopy became the source of water, enough to cause the fearful flood.

The answer to the second question, "where did the water go?", is also found in the Bible and the evidence for its truth is all around us. The Bible tells us that the water covered all the existing mountains at that time, referred to in Genesis as high hills, to a depth of 15 cubits: "and all the high hills that were under the whole heaven were covered. Fifteen cubits upward did the waters prevail" (Gen 7:19,20).

Let us remember that the earth was different before the flood. It never rained before the flood as we are told in the Bible:

"... for the LORD God had not caused it to rain upon the earth, but there went up a mist from the earth and watered the whole face of the ground" (Gen 2:5-6).

There were no high mountains, no mention of gale winds, snow or rain before the flood. They had no part to play in the perfect world God created. The climate was temperate all around the earth as evidenced by the fossil record.

Once the topography had been levelled by the devastating flood waters, and the world completely inundated, then great mountain uplifts began to take place.

"Thou coveredst it (the earth) with the deep as with a garment: the waters stood above the mountains. At thy rebuke they fled; at the voice of thy thunder they hasted away. They go up by the mountains, they go down by the valleys (the mountains go up; the valleys go down) unto the place which thou hast founded for them " (Ps 104:6-8).

Thus the present mountain ranges of the world were formed during or after the flood. The evidence for this is overwhelming:

- Geologists consider most of the great mountainous areas to have been uplifted since man has been on the earth.
- That these areas have been under water is clear from the fact that, near the summits, they are formed largely of marine strata often containing recent marine fossils.
- Although the mechanism of mountain formation is still a subject of controversy among geophysicists, the tremendous energies associated with the eruptions and erosions of the great flood provide the most logical model within which to find the true answer.
- The great mountain uplifts and corresponding ocean basin depressions, would necessarily be accompanied by an abundance of other tectonic activities such as faults, folds, thrusts and earth movements of many kinds. The present earthquake belt and continuing earthquake activities around the world can be understood as remnant effects of the great post-diluvian uplifts.
- The same applies to the earth's significant volcanism: the eruptions of the fountains of the deep (Gen 7:11). The post-flood isostatic readjustments, especially the mountain uplifts, would surely have triggered the release of additional floods of magma, and these are reflected in the tremendous recent lava plains around the world, as well as the great number of only recently extinct volcanoes, not to mention the considerable number still alive.

Another aspect is the depth to which mountains were covered. The Bible tells us that the flood waters prevailed to a height of 15 cubits above the earth. Amazingly if one calculates the draught of

Noah's ark when loaded, the result is 15 cubits ! God is telling us today that He made sure the ark floated safely over the highest mountains without even scratching the lowest piece of gopher wood. What a wonderful God we have who is interested in every detail of our lives.

The Bible tells us that the ark landed on the mountains of Ararat. The climate soon changed as we shall discuss later on and snow began to fall. Eventually the mountain became encased with a permanent ice cap and the ark itself has perhaps been preserved in ice for thousands of years as a silent monument to God's judgement on a wicked world.

From time to time through the intervening centuries, during periods of occasional melt back, travellers have reported seeing the vessel projecting through the ice cap. These reports became so numerous and convincing that a long series of expeditions began to venture forth to locate the ark. These have all proved difficult and dangerous both from the nature of the mountain and the political turmoil in the area around it [1].

Whether anyone will find Noah's ark, depends on whether the Lord wishes to reveal it to the world at this time. However, this does not affect our faith in the word of God. Noah's ark is a reality because it is in the Bible.

Once again the message for believers is to take the word of God literally, it is perfect in every detail. True science agrees with the account of the flood. The evidence is all around us: for a universal catastrophic flood, several thousand years ago; for a perfectly designed ark capable of withstanding the extreme conditions described in Genesis and carrying Noah and his family and two of each kind of animal safely till the flood waters receded; for a different atmosphere capable of revealing God's promise: the rainbow. The evidence is as clear as daylight, and those who choose not to believe are without excuse.

REFERENCES

1. Morris, J.D. *Noah's Ark and the Ararat Adventure*, Master Books Colorado Springs, USA, 1994.

Chapter 17
EVIDENCE AND MORE EVIDENCE

The flood as described in the book of Genesis forms an essential part of the Bible. Sadly evolutionists and many Christians today do not accept the account of a universal flood and of Noah's ark. They reject it, supposedly on scientific grounds.

When examined with an open mind that has not been brainwashed by false theories, all the evidence supports a universal flood as detailed in the Bible. We shall consider some examples.

I. Fossils

Fossils are formed when a living creature is entrapped and buried quickly in swirling sediment without being exposed to natural decay, scavenging or disintegration.

Therefore the mere existence of fossils is evidence of catastrophic death by water. Consequently, the existence of graveyards of fossils all over the world is evidence of a catastrophe on the scale explained in the Bible, a universal flood .

Let us consider some of the statements made by scientists on the fossil findings which show the great extent of this catastrophe:

Velikkovsky, in his book *Earth In Upheaval* writes:

"When a fish dies its body floats on the surface or sinks to the bottom and is devoured rather quickly, actually in a matter of hours, by other fish. However, the fossil fish found in sedimentary rocks is very often preserved with all its bones intact. Entire shoals of fish over large areas, numbering billions of specimen, are found in a state of agony, but with no mark of scavenger attack" [1].

Heribert-Nilsson of the Swedish Botanical Institute writes : "In pieces of amber, which may reach a size of 5 kilos or more, insects and parts of flowers are preserved, even the most fragile structures ... it is quite astounding to find they belong to all regions of the earth ..." [2].

There are examples all over the world of such findings:[3]

- Fossil graveyards in Nebraska with thousands of bones of fossil mammals in a layer that runs horizontally in a limestone hill, evidently water-laid. Fossils of rhinos, camels, giant boars and numerous other exotic animals are found jumbled together.
- More than a billion herring fossils averaging 15-20 cm (6-8 inches) in length, on 4 square miles in California.
- La Brea pits in Los Angeles with tens of thousands of specimens of all kinds of living and extinct animals (each of which, by the unbelievable uniformitarian explanation, fell into this sticky graveyard by accident one at a time!).
- The Sicilian hippopotamus beds, the great mammal beds of the Rockies, the dinosaur beds of the Black Hills and the Rockies as well as in the Gobi desert, are but a few examples of this universal graveyard: a morbid evidence of God's judgement of this earth by the flood in the days of Noah.

2. Sedimentary Rocks

Almost all of the sedimentary rocks of the earth, which are the ones containing fossils, have been laid down by moving waters. This statement is so obvious and so universally accepted that it needs neither proof nor elaboration. Sedimentary rocks by definition are those that have been deposited as sediments. The Oxford dictionary defines such rocks as "earthy or detrital matter deposited by aqueous agency". Obviously those great masses of sediment must first have been eroded from some previous location, transported, and then deposited, exactly the sort of thing which occurs in any flood and which must have occurred on a uniquely grand scale during the great flood of Genesis.

3. Polystrate Fossils

As discussed in a previous section, polystrate fossils are fossils of animals and plants, especially tree trunks, extending through several strata often six metres (twenty feet) or more in thickness. According to evolution, these strata take millions of years to be deposited. Yet fossils of trees standing vertically or upside down extend through three to four layers!

It is beyond question that this type of fossil must have been buried quickly or it would not have been preserved intact while the strata accumulated around it over the alleged millions of years. The only way to explain such polystrate fossils is by the action of the great flood and hence their existence is further evidence for the Genesis flood.

4. Geologic Faults

The geologic column, which is described by geologists as a regular succession of rock layers starting with the oldest at the bottom and the youngest at the top, is nowhere found as predicted. Vast areas of older rocks are found *on top* of younger ones stretching for hundreds of square miles, so huge and laid down so smoothly that they can not be explained away as geologic faults. [4]

5. Footprints of Man and Dinosaurs

This brings us to the famous Paluxy River basin in Texas where footprints of man and dinosaur have been found and where a heated debate has been taking place over the authenticity of those human footprints. It is understandable that evolutionists are keen to discredit such evidence because if dinosaurs and human beings walked together on this earth just before the Genesis flood 4-5 thousand years ago, then evolution will have to take its rightful place as the greatest deceit in the history of mankind.

The excavations at Glen Rose and the Paluxy River have been going on for a number of years, and a Creation Evidences Museum has been erected near the excavations site. All recent excavations have been documented in the presence of the media and independent qualified observers to avoid a repeat of the allegations of fabricating the evidence. [5]

Over 50 human footprints and many more dinosaur footprints have been excavated. The left/right pattern of walk is consistent. Some of the footprints (41 cm, or 16 inches) are larger than the average human foot size today reminding us of the verse in Genesis " there were giants in the earth in those days" (Gen 6:4). At the same level were found a human tooth, a fossilized human finger, and many other fossils which according to evolution lived hundreds of millions of years apart!

Excavations are still going on as more human footprints are found. The hope is that as more people watch the process of excavation and the findings, they will be able to find freedom from evolutionary brainwashing.

Russian scientists reported finding 1500 tracks made by dinosaurs in Turkmania, and among them were human footprints. The reports concluded that such findings will "create a revolution in the science of man. Humanity would grow older thirty fold and its history would be at least 150 million years long." [6]

The ridiculous length evolutionists go to in order to keep the theory of Evolution alive! Well as far as we are concerned this is further evidence that dinosaurs and man lived together having been created together on day number six and their footprints in various places is evidence of their desperate flight from the wrath of God during the Genesis flood.

6. Climatic Changes

Noah and his family walked out of the ark to a new world. The rainbow was seen for the first time after the rain as a sign from God that He will not flood the whole earth again with water. The shielding from harmful radiation had diminished, the atmospheric pressure was less, the oxygen content was less ... and all this had an awful effect on Noah, his family and the animals.

The universal temperate climate, evidenced by the universal spread of fossil plants and animals before the flood, ceased to exist giving rise to extreme temperatures. Ice and snow fell without warning.

Fred Hoyle, among other outstanding meteorologists and astronomers, has recognised that extreme temperatures would arise as a result of the reduction of water vapour in the atmosphere. In his book *Frontiers of Astronomy* he writes:

"Evidently then an ice-age would arise if the greenhouse effect of our atmosphere were destroyed. This would happen if the concentrations of those gases of the atmosphere that are responsible for blocking the infra-red radiation were appreciably reduced. The gas of main importance in this respect is water vapour. The question therefore arises as to how the amount of water vapour in the atmosphere might be systematically reduced, especially the amount at a height of some 6,000 m (20,000 ft) above the ground. In this may lie the answer to the riddle of the ice age." [7]

Hence logically the effect of the disappearance of the canopy during the flood, is the sudden freezing in places where the fossil record indicates a previously more temperate climate.

One fascinating evidence for this is the tens of thousands of dead and frozen mammoths in Siberia [8]. Some of these have been discovered frozen and completely intact with their meals still in their stomachs indicating sudden death by freezing. Two Russian scientists who found the remains of a group of mammoths on an island off north-eastern Siberia claim that these have died only 4,000 years ago and not 10,000 as previously assumed. Dr Adrian Lister of London University admitted recently that there had been a mistake. The frantic reassessment of mammoth history has been called one "of the hottest stories in palaeontology".

Another more fascinating evidence is the recent discovery of iceman in the Alps in 1991. *Time* magazine issue of October 1992 had a detailed report of what they called "a discovery that stirred passion and controversy". The iceman was discovered as the snow melted partly in the Alps at the borders between Austria and Italy - "his discovery has already upset some long-held notions about the late stone age", reported *Time* magazine; while Dr Lawrence Barfield, at the department of Archaeology in Birmingham University said,"it seems almost that this find has been designer-made to embarrass the prehistorians" [8].

The body was dressed, had a haircut and tattoos. He was carrying sophisticated equipment, knew about leatherworks, had feathered arrows with sophisticated design, a bow that spanned 1.8m (5ft 10 inches) and a 99% pure copper axe! In his rucksack he had mushrooms used as antibiotics.

This astounded scientists who did not think that people at that time were so advanced. But the Bible tells us about men before the flood: Jabal, dwelling in tents and having cattle; Jubal handled the harp and organ; and Tubal-Cain, instructor in brass, copper and iron (Gen 4:20-22). The world had reached a level of sophistication at the time the iceman lived, and the discovery confirmed it.

The iceman was dated between 4600 years and 5300 years ago by carbon dating methods. Keeping in mind the over estimation of dates over 4000 years old by carbon dating, as recorded by Dr Libby himself the Nobel award winner in this field and the one who invented this method, we can explain the death by freezing of this healthy young man by the sudden change in climate as a result of the Genesis flood.

REFERENCES

1. Velikkovsky, I. *Earth In Upheaval*, Doubleday and Co., New York, 1955, p. 222.
2. Heribert-Nilsson, N. Synthetische Artbildung, pp. 1194-1195.
3. Whitcomb, J.C. and Morris, H.M. *The Genesis Flood,* Presbyterian and Reformed Publishing Company, New Jersey, USA, 1993, pp. 160-161.
4. ibid. pp. 180-200.
5. Baugh, C.E. and Wilson, C.A. *Dinosaur*, Promise Publishing Co., CA, 1987.
6. Robstov, C. "Tracking Dinosaurs", *Moscow News*, No. **24**, 1983, p. 10.
7. Hoyle, F. *Frontiers of Astronomy*, Harpers, New York, 1955, p. 8.
8. Whitcomb, J.C. *The World that Perished*, Baker Book House, Michigan, 1993, pp. 76-81.
9. Jaroff, L. "Iceman", *Time Magazine*, No. **43**, October 26, 1992, pp. 56-60.

Chapter 18
THE MYSTERY OF THE DINOSAURS

Those who accept the authority and integrity of the word of God have no problem believing that God created man and dinosaur on the *same* day. We are told in Genesis that on the sixth day of the creation week God "made the beast of the earth " and on the same day "God said, Let us make man in our image, after our likeness" (Gen 1:25,26).

Yet we are confronted by the statement that dinosaurs died away 70 million years before man arrived on the scene. Such ideas are propagated and promoted aggressively by teachers, books, scientific journals, programmes on radio and television, and even children's stories. We are told that this is fact - it is what scientists have agreed on - it is taught with complete authority.

I would like to assure the reader that there is no evidence from science that dinosaurs lived *millions* of years ago. We have seen in the previous chapters that the dating methods used lack all scientific credibility and the only reason evolutionists choose the millions and billions is the fact that without them evolution is a dead theory.

Some of the questions people ask when the subject of dinosaurs comes up are:

- If dinosaurs were so powerful why is there no mention of them in the Bible ?
- How could the dinosaurs fit in Noah's ark ?
- How and why did the dinosaurs die out ?

I shall give the answers to these questions from the scientific evidence and the word of God.

The name "dinosaur" was given to those huge fossils that have been uncovered by the palaeontologists. Consequently, one does not expect to find the same word in the Bible. However, this does not mean that those huge animals are not mentioned in the Bible. We read in the book of Job about an animal called *behemoth*. If one studies the description of behemoth carefully, one concludes without any

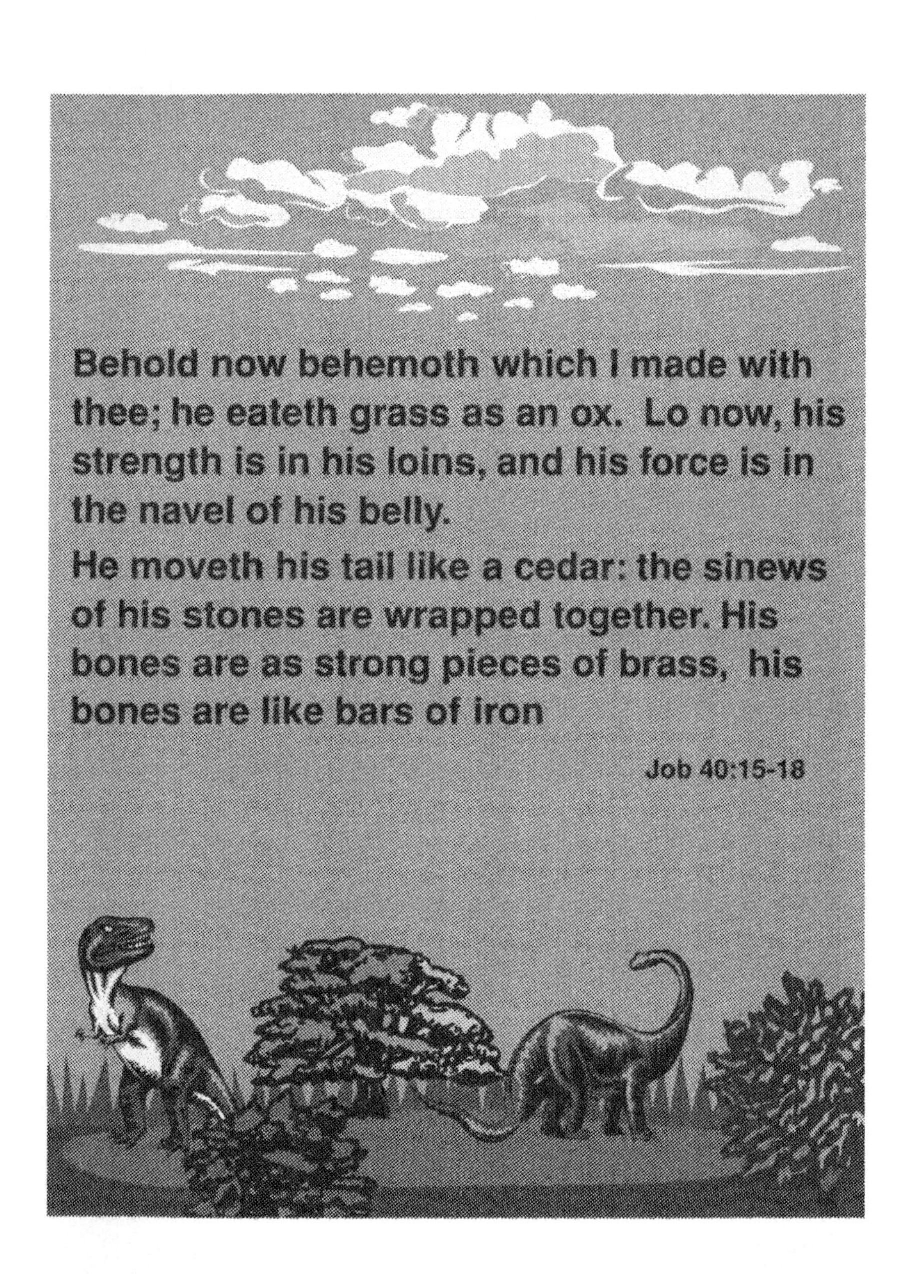

Figure 15: Dinosaur or Behemoth!

doubt that it is a dinosaur. Job 40 provides the necessary details:

1. "Behold now behemoth, which I made with thee..." (Job 40:15). Beyond any question, the word of God is consistent and clear: Job (man) and behemoth (dinosaur) were created together, on the same day: "which I made with thee!"

2. "He moveth his tail like a cedar: the sinews of his stones are wrapped together" (Job 40:17). Some commentators say that behemoth is an elephant, but the tail of the elephant is nothing like a cedar tree! The cedar tree points *upwards*. If evolutionists, and in particular natural history museum officials, read their Bibles, they would have known from the book of Job that the tail of the dinosaur is pointing upwards like the cedar. This would have saved them the embarrassment of having had to close all the natural history museums around the world a few years ago in order to turn the tails of the dinosaurs the right way up! They had the tail of the dinosaur down at first. Then they discovered that if the tail was down and it is so heavy it would have left 'tailprints' where Dinosaur footprints were found. Since they could not find such prints they decided the tail must point up! The second part of the verse describes so accurately the plates that covered some dinosaurs and looked like stones wrapped together.

3. "His bones are as strong pieces of brass; his bones are like bars of iron" (Job 40:18). This is a very accurate description of the strength of the bones of the dinosaur as revealed by the excavated fossils.

4. "He is the chief of the ways of God" (Job 40:19). Everyone agrees that the dinosaurs were the biggest animals in existence. Job was probably looking at what we call today Brachiosaurus, which weighed about 90 tons and was about 25 m (80 feet) long. Surely he is the chief of the ways of God!

5. "He drinketh up a river, and hasteneth not..." (Job 40:23). This verse describes the size of this animal and the fact that the dinosaur walked slowly due to its great weight.

6. "... his nose pierceth through snares" (Job 40:24). A particular feature of Brachiosaurus was the fact that his nostrils were not out on the end of his nose, or snout, like most other animals, but were located in a bony dome on top of his head.

I believe that anyone reading the description of behemoth in Job will have no doubt that the true name of the dinosaur is behemoth. It is interesting also to note that the name comes from two words combined together which in one language used in the Old Testament days (Arabic) mean "in him is death"! What a contrast to the description of the Lord Jesus "... in him was life" (John 1:4).

The second question is about Noah's ark and how could the dinosaurs fit in. We have seen in Chapter 15 that there was plenty of room in the Ark for two of each kind of animal including dinosaurs. One of the three levels of the ark, built according to the instruction of God to Noah in Genesis, could have taken them all. Keep in mind that Noah did not have to take on board the very huge dinosaurs. He would have probably taken in young and healthy specimens.

The third question is: how did the dinosaurs die out? Evolutionists have a problem answering this question. Over the years they have come up with more than *twenty* theories about how the dinosaurs died out. Every time a new study came out, it showed how unscientific the previous theory had been, before proposing its own ideas. Recently in *Time Magazine* and the *National Geographic Magazine* [1] some evolutionists had to admit that the most logical answer is that dinosaurs must have died out by a natural catastrophe like a flood. For obvious reasons they do not mention Noah or the book of Genesis!

We can explain the absence of huge dinosaurs today in a manner that agrees with true science. Science tells us that dinosaurs are "terrible lizards". Lizards, unlike other animals, keep growing in size as long as they are alive. Human beings, for example, grow taller until the age of about 18, when they stop growing taller even if they live till they are 100. The Bible explains how after the flood Noah and all the animals came out to a different world. The vapour canopy (the waters above) from Genesis 1:7 emptied all its contents on the earth during the flood. We are told that God shortened the life of man to almost one tenth of what it was before the flood (Gen 6:3). We assume that animal life was shortened accordingly and hence a dinosaur which lived for say 100 years before the flood and grew to a height of 15 m (50 ft), would live for say 10-20 years after the flood and hence grow to a height of say 1.5-3 m (5-10 ft). This explains scientifically the disappearance of huge dinosaurs, and the fact that there are large dragon-lizards, of the dinosaur kind, in places like the Indonesian island of Komodo, with a size of over 3 m (10 ft) ! [2]

Another major change after the flood was the reduction of oxygen content and atmospheric pressure as discussed in Chapter 14. The effect of this change is detrimental on huge dinosaurs. The fossil record shows that dinosaurs have a small chest capacity relative to their huge bodies. Consequently with reduced oxygen content and lower atmospheric pressure after the flood, it would have been far more difficult for oxygen to reach *all* parts of their bodies. This would have resulted in the big dinosaurs finding it very difficult to survive, and they would die out.

As far as true science is concerned there is no problem with accepting the account of creation as it appears literally in the book of Genesis. God created man and dinosaur on the same day; they both went into Noah's ark; came out to a changed world; lived shorter lives. Consequently, dinosaurs did not grow to the same sort of gigantic size which was normal in the days before the flood. As Christians we have all the answers to give to those who question the authority of the Bible and to those who teach our children and young people wrong things about the dinosaurs, trying to use such stories to shake or mock their trust in the word of God.

We cannot compromise with evolution on any matter even if it sounds as simple as the dinosaurs. If we allow teachers and authors to teach children that the dinosaurs died away 70 million years before man arrived at the scene, then these children will not trust the Bible nor the God of the Bible, who from what they have been taught, knows nothing about science. They will reject the Bible and lose an opportunity of knowing about the Saviour, which might not come their way again. We have to stand firm and make the truth known at every possible occasion "... in season and out of season " (2 Tim 4:2).

REFERENCES

1. Gore, R. "Dinosaurs", *National Geographic Magazine,* Vol. **183**, No. **1**, January 1993, p. 26.
2. Whitcomb, J.C. *The World that Perished*, Baker Book House, Michigan, 1993, pp. 30-31.

Chapter 19
THE SILENT WITNESS

There is a silent witness in the rocks of the earth. All around the world, underneath our feet, from the deepest ocean floors to the highest mountain peaks, there is a vast cemetery containing the remains of animals and plants that once existed and flourished on this earth.

Modern speculation under the misleading umbrella of science has managed to distort the testimony of this graveyard into a fictional record of slow evolutionary development over millions of years.

Sadly this is what is being taught and accepted today as a scientific fact in most educational establishments around the world. This same notion has also infiltrated many christian organisations today, resulting in panic compromise theories to incorporate evolution in the first chapter of Genesis.

However, the silent witness in the earth speaks of death and destruction not development; extinction not evolution! If we are honest with the evidence and interpret it correctly it testifies of a powerful Creator who controls and judges His creation. When He decided to send the fearful flood, God (described in the Bible as a God of power and of love, of judgement and of mercy) did not forget man. When He judged the world that then was, He did not forget His mercy. We are reminded of the Psalmist who, when he considered the greatness of our Creator, had to exclaim: "What is man that thou art mindful of him?" (Psalm 8:4).

When God decided to send the flood, He provided a means of escape for those who had faith to believe His word: the ark. In the event, of all the human race, only Noah and his family entered the ark and escaped the wrath of God.

In the same Bible we read those words spoken by our Creator, the Lord Jesus Christ Himself: "as the days of Noah were, so shall also the coming of the Son of man be. For as in the days that were before the flood they were eating and drinking, marrying and giving in marriage, until the day that Noah entered into the ark, and knew not until the flood came, and took them all away; so shall also the coming of the Son of man be" (Mat 24:37-39).

We have seen the accuracy of the Bible. God will judge this earth as He promised and only those who enter the ark will be safe. But the ark this time is none other than the Lord Jesus Christ, the Son of God. He left His glories in heaven and came to this earth of ours to show us the love that He and His Father have for us: "For God so loved the world that he gave his only begotten Son that whosoever believeth in him should not perish" (as they perished during the flood) "but have everlasting life " (John 3:16).

He paid the price for our salvation by dying at the cross of Calvary in our place nearly two thousand years ago. Today, with arms wide open He is calling everyone: "Come unto me, all ye that labour and are heavy laden, and I will give you rest " (Mat 11:28).

In the days of Noah, at a time known only to Himself, God shut the door. The opportunity for those who were outside was gone forever. Don't miss the opportunity this time. Don't let false science be your passport to a fearful eternity. Make sure you are safe inside.

PART IV - WRITTEN THAT YOU MIGHT BELIEVE

Chapter 20
LET US REASON

"Come now, and let us reason together, saith the LORD" (Isa 1:18).

"How long halt ye between two opinions? If the LORD be God, follow him" (1 Kings 18:21).

If you were still undecided whether to take the Bible seriously when you first picked up this book and you were reluctant to take a stand on the creation issue - this chapter is written for you.

If you made a confession of faith in your youth, only to find out as you went to university that your science books seemed to contradict what you had always thought was the truth; if you then started doubting your faith and found yourself going so quickly away from God that you thought you "lost your faith" - this chapter is for you.

If you have been brought up in a christian home, attended church meetings, felt unable to argue or discuss problems and contradictions you thought existed between your way of thinking and the Bible - this chapter is written for you.

You must have seen that there is overwhelming evidence from science to support the authority of the Bible and to contradict evolution. This evidence has been presented to you in order that you might think seriously about the Bible and about your Creator.

If we have been created as the Bible tells us, then this Creator owns us and He sets the rules. He has told us in detail how we can be reconciled to Him after sin has separated us from a holy God. He has set it out very clearly for us in the Bible: "That if thou shalt confess with thy mouth the Lord Jesus, and shalt believe in thine heart that

God hath raised him from the dead, thou shalt be saved" (Rom 10:9). Having seen the accuracy of the Bible in scientific issues, how can we ignore its warnings concerning our spiritual welfare? The Bible warns about hell: it must be a reality; it is not a mediaeval concept as leading evolutionists would claim. The Lord Jesus Himself talked about a real place of torment: "... the rich man also died, and was buried; And in hell he lift up his eyes, being in torments ..." (Luke 16:22,23). Do not ignore the warnings to your certain and sure destruction. I plead with you not to gamble with your precious soul.

I challenge you today with the words of Elijah "If the LORD be God follow him" (1 Kings 18:21). If you haven't taken this step yet, you can take it now. Confess to the Lord that you have sinned, for the Bible tells us clearly that *all* have sinned. We have all broken God's commands and refused to accept His plan for our salvation. "All we like sheep have gone astray; we have turned every one to his own way; and the LORD hath laid on him the iniquity of us all" (Isa 53:6). Repent, that means to make a complete U- turn, with your back now to sin and your eyes fixed on the Lord Jesus Christ who died in your place at the cross nearly two thousand years ago. He satisfied God's demands on your life and opened the way for you to be able to commune with a holy God without fear. We know that this is true because God "raised him up from the dead, and gave him glory" and "a name which is above every name: That at the name of Jesus every knee should bow, of things in heaven, and things in earth, and things under the earth; And that every tongue should confess that Jesus Christ is Lord, to the glory of God the Father" (1 Pet 1:21; Phil 2:9-11). Ask Him to forgive you your sins and come and live in your heart. The Lord Jesus promised in the same Bible: "him that cometh to me I will in no wise cast out" (John 6:37). He promised to make you a new creation fit for eternal life, washed by His blood. He promised to come one day to take us to be with Him forever: " I go to prepare a place for you. And if I go and prepare a place for you, I will come again, and receive you unto myself; that where I am, there ye may be also" (John 14:2,3). That place is heaven. God is asking you: "Why will ye die?" (Ezek 33:11).

If you have accepted the Lord as your Saviour in the past, but have gone cold and quiet due to the problems of evolution and the doubt that Satan brings into your life through it, it is time to renew your commitment and to stand up and be counted. Lift up your head for our Creator is great. Trust in His word and the enemy will be defeated by the word of God. You have to put your trust in God and His word, the Bible, to be able to tell the enemy "It is written!!" and the Lord will restore unto you the joy of His salvation (Ps 51:12).

If you were born in a christian home, your parent's desire is for you to be saved and to know their wonderful Saviour. They pray for you to be saved and will do all they can to stop you from going to hell. Do you expect them to behave differently if they love you?

If you have been disappointed by the behaviour of some who say they are Christians but live a life that does not match what they teach, turn your eyes to the cross: "Looking unto Jesus the author and finisher of our faith" (Heb 12:2). The Lord Jesus is the only one to follow for He "suffered for us, leaving us an example, that ye should follow his steps" (1 Pet 2:21). Then you will never be disappointed.

This book should help you answer any queries on the authority of the word of God regarding scientific issues. If the Bible is perfect in scientific matters as we have seen, how can we doubt its accuracy in spiritual matters. There will always be things we cannot understand with our finite human minds. But God has revealed to us in His word that "... his divine power hath given unto us all things that pertain unto life and godliness, through the knowledge of him that hath called us to glory and virtue: Whereby are given unto us exceeding great and precious promises" (2 Pet 1:3,4). It is now your responsibility: "choose ye today".

Chapter 21
STAND UP AND BE COUNTED

"Have not I written to thee excellent things in counsels and knowledge. That I might make thee know the certainty of the words of truth; that thou mightest answer the words of truth to them that send unto thee" (Prov 22:20,21).

First night at the Proms at the Royal Albert Hall in London 1996, and the orchestra was performing Haydn's *Creation*. The commentator explained how daily before composing, Haydn prayed that the music would somehow reflect the greatness and majesty of God in creation.

During the intermission, the BBC took us on a trip to explain that people do not believe in creation today. We were told that scientists *know* that the universe came about by the Big Bang!

They also interviewed a number of people who supported that view. Then it came to the Bishop of Oxford to give the christian view on the subject. He said, "We know that the first few chapters of Genesis are myth!"

If the broadcasters and many scientists are not ashamed to stand by the flimsy Big Bang theory; if some nominal church leaders are not ashamed to proclaim in public that the creation account in the Bible is myth; why are we ashamed to stand up for our faith and proclaim to the world our complete trust in the authority and integrity of the whole Bible, from Genesis to Revelation, as the perfect word of God?

One of the most frequent questions I am asked at the end of a talk on this subject is: why hasn't anyone told me this before? Young believers struggle with their faith against the claims of their teachers and friends and they are ignored when they search for answers. I heard recently as I was writing this section that a 16-year old student brought up in a christian home suddenly told his parents he does not believe in God any more. At the bottom of it all was the issue of evolution taught as scientific fact in his school. Only when he read some articles about creation versus evolution did he realise that the Bible is perfect and he had nothing to be afraid of. This resulted in the young man being on fire for his Lord. We need to share the *facts* with as many people as possible. We need to come out clearly and boldly on the side of our Creator irrespective of what people say or think. We must be ready always to give an answer to everyone who asks.

After hearing what was presented at one of the talks I gave, a university graduate who has been practising occupational therapy to help people walk again after accidents or illnesses, was shocked. She said, "If what you say is true I can understand why we are not succeeding". She went on to explain that the whole theory on which her work is based assumes that human beings evolved from apes, and hence used to walk on all fours. Therapists consequently base their therapy on a process of development from walking on four legs to walking on two. If evolution is not correct then we never walked on four and the therapy does not produce the desired results because it is not based on scientific evidence. This is one penalty humanity has to pay for believing a lie!

Another medical person working in the same field said that a certain doctor wrote, answering a query about the walking disability of one of his patients. He explained that: "The basic fact is that as humans we are yet to be fully adapted to the two-legged posture!" (reference withheld for confidentiality). It makes you wonder how many millions of years does that person need to wait to get over this disability. It begs the question: Is there any science left even in such fields? We are living in the final days when people "shall turn away their ears from the truth, and shall be turned unto fables", and the exhortation for us is "watch thou in all things" (2 Tim 4:4,5).

The truth is in our hands: "Thy word is truth" (John 17:17). Let us stand up and be counted. There are many out there being deceived every day by teachers, professors, books, magazines, radio and television programmes covering all sorts of subjects. Paul writes about this to Timothy warning him about people in the last days: "Ever learning, and never able to come to the knowledge of the truth ... But they shall proceed no further: for their folly shall be manifest unto all men" (2 Tim 3:7,9). It is up to us to make their folly manifest unto all, before they mislead more people to believe the lie!

Chapter 22
LESSONS FROM SCIENCE

"And Solomon answered all her questions. ... And she said to the king: ... Blessed be the LORD thy God" (2 Chron 9:2,5,8).

The Lord has taught me over the years as I studied this subject, to accept *everything* that is in the Bible without interpreting it to suit my own ideas and opinions, whatever their source may be.

I have learnt that if I take the Bible seriously, then there is no problem in accepting the truths that are recorded there: God created us in His own image, in six literal days several thousand years ago, to live with Him. We have all "sinned and come short of the glory of God" (Rom 3:23). God's love is so great that He sent the Lord Jesus to die at the cross of Calvary in our place. The Bible tells me that I must repent and accept the Lord Jesus as my own personal Saviour to have forgiveness of sins and everlasting life. Then, and only then, I must obey His command and be baptised. Having been baptised, and having testified to the world that the Lord Jesus is now first in my new life, I must without delay remember Him in His own appointed way by breaking bread with believers: "This do in remembrance of me" (Luke 22:19).

If we take the word of God literally then we know that one of the main reasons He keeps us in this world is to win souls. Why then is this experience becoming so rare? Why are so many of our local churches suffering from decreasing numbers, and in some sad cases closing down altogether? Why are some of our young people, especially after going through university, leaving the assemblies?

I believe the answer to all these questions lies in the fact that we have stopped taking the Bible literally. We are happy to compromise with the world in almost every aspect of our new life. The Lord wants to bless us. He wants to do miracles in our midst, the greatest miracle of all: the salvation of the human soul. Let us be truthful before the Lord: when was the last time we brought a soul to the Saviour? When did we last witness the birth of a new creation?

Why is this becoming so rare? The Lord is the same. He wants people to be saved and this is why He went all the way to the cross. The problem is in us. We read in Joshua 3:5: "Sanctify yourselves: for tomorrow the LORD will do wonders among you". Holiness is a prerequisite for miracles.

The world and worldliness have entered every aspect of our lives and the Lord wants us to take His word seriously before He performs miracles in our midst. "The friendship of the world is enmity with God" (James 4:4). These are very strong words that we ignore so many times in our lives. We are guilty of standing in the way of revivals.

Let us illustrate this with one or two examples. Take the issue of dress. We often say it is not important, and end up wearing things that bring shame to the name of our Lord. But if we consider the fact that God killed the first animal in history, the first sacrifice was aimed at providing coats for Adam and Eve, to replace the fig leaves: "Unto Adam also and to his wife did the LORD God make coats of skins, and clothed them"(Gen 3:21). The word for coats is the same one used for Aaron's coats; clothes that cover the whole body. Once again the basis of dress is recorded in Genesis, and explained and expounded in the New Testament teaching about decency and modesty (1 Tim 2:9). How many christian believers today have gone back to the fig leaves, ignoring all the teachings in the Bible about decency and modesty, just because we do not want to be different from the rest of the society.

Or take the subject of alcoholic drinks, which is discussed and justified by many, including those who are supposed to be examples to others. If we as believers want to ignore the great number of verses that warn us against drink and being in the company of those who drink, how can we ignore the teaching about not being a stumbling block, knowing that the Lord himself warned us that "whosoever shall offend one of these little ones that believe in me, it is better for him that a millstone were hanged about his neck, and he were cast into the sea" (Mark 9:42). These are very solemn words: they are God's words recorded for us in the Bible. We try to go along with the world in an attempt to prove to them as some put it "that we are normal human beings". We forget that as children of the King of kings and Lord of lords, "we are ambassadors for Christ" (2 Cor 5:20), "a chosen generation, a royal priesthood, an holy nation, a peculiar people; that ye should show forth the praises of him who hath called you out of darkness into his marvellous light" (1 Pet 2:9). Therefore we should "walk in wisdom toward them that are without, redeeming the time" (Col 4:5).

These two simple examples illustrate how we defy the authority of the word of God to do what our old nature still requires of us, and thus conform to the world. Let us examine our lives against God's standards and not against what is acceptable to society. When we as individuals and as assemblies of God's people humble ourselves before the Lord and ask Him to examine our lives and "see if there be any wicked way in me, and lead me in the way everlasting" (Ps 139:24), when we as God's people take His word literally and apply it to every aspect of our lives, asking His forgiveness and His Holy Spirit to take control of our lives, then the Lord will do miracles in our midst and souls will be saved, not one every year, but a great harvest as He promised us in His Book. Assemblies will then grow in number by new birth and not by migration, and the presence of the Lord will be evident in our midst.

Let us as believers start with our own lives, surrendering everything into the hands of the One who loved us to the uttermost. Let us as companies of God's people spend more time on our knees asking specifically for help and guidance to live a life of holiness, "for this is the will of God, your sanctification" (1 Thess 4:3). If we fail sometimes, let us not bring God's standards down with us in order to justify ourselves, but rather on our knees ask for forgiveness and strength to live once again the victorious life through the power of the Holy Spirit of God who dwells in us. Let us then plead with the Lord for the souls that are passing every day into a lost eternity, amongst them members of our families, friends and people whom we love. The Lord has often challenged me with the fact that if I *really* believe in a literal hell, how can I keep quiet about it when people cross my path every day?

As believers, let us redeem the time (Eph 5:16). We must preach the gospel in season and out of season: it is *always* the right time to preach the gospel for "woe is unto me, if I preach not the gospel" (1 Cor 9:16)! Sadly, in so many cases we have replaced gospel preaching with social work and 'bridge building'. Our priorities and outreach methods are shifting from scriptural basis to human management and marketing skills and then we wonder why people are not saved. I always think if Noah decided to use his own judgement and skill to 'improve' on the dimensions of the ark that God gave him, what a rough time all on board would have had! There is no alternative to complete obedience to the word of God if we want to live according to His will. When in doubt about something let us not take risks but be happy to sacrifice anything for the Lord and avoid the risk of grieving the Holy Spirit. There is "a crown of glory" (1 Pet 5:4) awaiting us. There is a time when "every one of us shall give account of himself to God" (Rom 14:12). Let us start *now*, for today is an accepted time. I believe that the Lord is challenging us, His people, at the close of this century. He demands a response. Let us lovingly and willingly present our bodies "a living sacrifice, holy, acceptable unto God" (Rom 12:1), for He will not stand at the door of our hearts and knock forever. Let us fix our eyes on the Lord Jesus and our hearts will then be lifted up in adoration and submission, "unto him that loved us, and washed us from our sins in his own blood" (Rev 1:5).

Chapter 23
CREATION AND THE NEW CREATION

"In the beginning God created the heaven and the earth" (Gen 1:1), "... if any man be in Christ, he is a new creature", or a new creation (2 Cor 5:17).

We are told in the Bible that: "All scripture is given by inspiration of God, and is profitable for ... instruction in righteousness" (2 Tim 3:16). There are further spiritual lessons for us today from the account of creation that will help us understand the new creation. The Bible tells us the Creator in both cases is the same: our Lord and Saviour Jesus Christ: "... by him were all things created" (Col 1:16).

When we consider the creation we cannot but praise the Creator and repeat with the Psalmist: "When I consider thy heavens the work of thy fingers, the moon and the stars, which thou hast ordained: What is man that thou art mindful of him?"(Ps 8:3,4).

When we consider the new creation, made possible by the blood of our Saviour shed at the cross of Calvary, we are overwhelmed with the love of the Creator; "Greater love hath no man than this, that a man lay down his life for his friends" (John 15:13).

We shall consider the similarities between the creation and the new creation and see what the Creator wants to impress on our hearts.

"In the beginning God created the heaven and the earth. And the earth was without form, and void; and darkness was upon the face of the deep" (Gen 1:1,2).

Isn't this a perfect picture of our condition before we met the Lord? Isn't this the picture of humanity: without form, empty and in total darkness! But, on this background the Spirit of God moved or hovered, like a dove hovers over the nest to see if it is the right time to come into the nest and fill it with life and warmth and protection. This is exactly what the Holy Spirit is doing: hovering over the nests of peoples' hearts who are without form and void and in darkness: convicting of sin, convincing that we cannot do anything towards our salvation, and presenting God's Son, the Lord Jesus Christ, as the only Saviour. When the right time comes and the heart responds in repentance and acceptance of the Lord Jesus as personal Saviour, then God's command is issued: "Let there be light", and the light chases away the darkness as the miracle of the new creation takes place. This is the ***first*** day of the believer's new life: "Behold all things are become new" (2 Cor 5:17).

On the ***second*** day God "...divided the waters which were under the firmament from the waters which were above the firmament" (Gen 1:7). Similarly the second day in our christian life is a time of separation.

This is a subject many preachers do not like talking about yet it is very clear and essential in our christian life. This might be a reaction to some who took separation to extremes, even not eating with their children, resulting in a generation of young people who are either suffering from the psychological effects of neglect by parents or rebelling against all religion. We are not talking about this kind of separation. We are talking about being in the world but "...not of the world" (John 15:19), showing love to all those we get in touch with, without compromising our christian principles. The world has entered our lives in so many ways and the Bible warns us against this: "Love not the world, neither the things that are in the world. If any man love the world, the love of the Father is not in him" (1 John 2:15).

The second day is a day of finding out that the will of the Lord in our life is our sanctification. "...present your bodies a living sacrifice, holy, acceptable unto God ... And be not conformed to this world: but be ye transformed" (Rom 12:1,2). "Know ye not that your body is the temple of the Holy Ghost ... for ye are bought with a price: therefore glorify God in your body" (1 Cor 6:19,20). "Come out from among them, and be ye separate, saith the Lord" (2 Cor 6:17). "Be ye holy, for I am holy" (1 Pet 1:16).

We need to know that there should be no deep fellowship between believers and non-believers. This is rightly taught to young people when thinking of a partner in their life. But what we miss today is teaching that relations between believers ought to be in complete purity: "keep thyself pure" (1 Tim 5:22), and "...it is good for a man not to touch a woman" (1 Cor 7:1), a verse which has been completely changed in some modern translations of the Bible (perhaps making such versions more popular for use in many places?).

Once we learn the lesson of separation of the second day we can move on to the ***third*** day. On the third day God created "... the fruit tree yielding fruit after his kind, whose seed is in itself" (Gen 1:11). And so the third day in the christian life is fruit-bearing.

Notice that the seed is in us. The fruits of believers are believers who are exactly like them: what a responsibility: "Be thou an example of the believers, in word, in conversation, in charity, in spirit, in faith, in purity" (1 Tim 4:12). The Lord is challenging us today: are we bearing fruit? When was the last time we led a lost soul to the cross for salvation and watched that fruit grow for the glory of our Saviour? If it is a very long time ago, we need to go back to the second day and review our lives against the will of our Lord and Saviour stated clearly in the Bible.

On the ***fourth*** day God created the sun, moon and stars. So the fourth day in our christian life is the time when our lives shine like stars.

We live in the heavenlies, but "...let your light so shine before men, that they may see your good works, and glorify your Father which is in heaven" (Matt 5:16). Like the moon we do not have light in us. We only reflect the light of the sun: our Lord and Saviour, our Creator; for He is "the light of the world" (John 8:12). But sometimes our light is not seen. This is the time when there is eclipse of the moon, which happens when the earth comes between the moon and the sun. Back to the second day! When the world comes between the believer and the Lord, the testimony is blurred and a partial eclipse occurs. If we do not remove the worldly obstacle, total eclipse will follow and our testimony will be marred. What a miserable situation for believers to be in. Let us be tuned to our Saviour, hear His voice alone and obey Him, "For ye are bought with a price" (1 Cor 6:20).

On the ***fifth*** day God created the birds and the fish. Both defy the laws of nature. A bird can fly although its weight is heavier than air and a fish can swim in great depths where the pressure would make it impossible to survive naturally. This is the fifth day of our christian life: a day of victory over the laws of nature.

We soar high into the heavenlies close to our Saviour's heart, and we explore the depth of His love and fellowship, and the treasures of His word. Notice that a bird needs a lot of effort to fly when there is no wind, but in the wind - one flap of the wings and the sky is the limit! Similarly, as believers, if we do not depend on the power of the Holy Spirit, we have to struggle a lot to achieve very little. But when we depend on the Holy Spirit we soar high into the heavenlies where the things on the earth that stood in our way will look so insignificant compared to the blessings of the nearness to our Lord and Saviour, our Creator and Redeemer.

And on the ***sixth*** day God crowned the creation by something special: "And God said, Let us make man in our image ... So God created man in his own image, in the image of God created he him" (Gen 1:26,27). When I read this, and consider that this same Creator sent His own Son to die on a cross to redeem man, I am overwhelmed by the love of God! I, a drop in the ocean of His vast universe, yet He cares for me so much! If we spend more time as believers thinking of this, our life and our priorities in life will change.

So the sixth day is the final day in our christian life on this earth. It is the time when we strive to be conformed to the image of God's Son (Rom 8:29). Someone once said that God was so pleased with His Son that He wanted a heaven full of people who looked exactly like Him! Our christian life is full of experiences. If we live it according to the will of the Lord, those experiences will mould us into the image that God wants us to be. The more conformed to His image we become, the more we can experience the abundant life and the happier will our departure be from the scene of this world when the Lord calls us home. I am reminded here of Stephen, who when they stoned him because of his bold stand for his Saviour, he being conformed to the image of God's Son, cried out like his Master: "Lord, lay not this sin to their charge" (Acts 7:60). What a glorious entry into glory he had: "Behold, I see the heavens opened, and the Son of man *standing* on the right hand of God" (Acts 7:56). What a wonderful hope to look forward to: one glorious day I shall see my Saviour "face to face" (1 Cor 13:12); I "shall be like him; for *I* shall see him as he is "(1 John 3:2). I shall be able to gaze at my Saviour's face and understand the meaning of "yea, he is altogether lovely" (Song 5:16). I shall be able to kneel down at His pierced feet and with Calvary in mind proclaim with the redeemed: Thou art worthy ... my Creator ... my Saviour ... my Lord and my God.

What a majestic start of an eternal ***seventh*** day, when "He rested from all his work which God created and made" (Gen 2:3). We shall be with Him forever. O the wonder of it all : Amen, come Lord Jesus: our Creator, our Saviour and our Lord.

RECOMMENDED BOOKS FOR FURTHER READING

Gish, D. *The Amazing Story of Creation*, Institute for Creation Research, CA, USA, 1990.

Gish, D.T. *Evolution: The fossils say NO!*, Creation Life Publishers, San Diego, 1979.

Ham, K., Snelling, A. and Wieland, C. *The Answers Book,* Master Books, El Cajon, CA, USA, 1992.

Lamont, A. *21 Great Scientists who Believed the Bible*, Creation Science Foundation, Brisbane, 1995.

Morris, H.M. *The Bible and Modern Science*, Moody Press, Chicago, 1968.

Morris, H.M. and Parker, G.E. *What is Creation Science?* (revised ed.), Master Books, El Cajon, California, 1987.

Morris, H.M. *The Biblical Basis for Modern Science,* Baker Book House, Michigan, 1993.

Rosevear, D. *Creation Science*, New Wine Press, England, 1991.

Whitcomb, J.C. and Morris, H.M. *The Genesis Flood*, Presbyterian and Reformed Publishing, 1961.

Whitcomb, J.C. *The World that Perished*, Baker Book House, Michigan, 1993.

Index